SAM35 YEARBOOK 16

Editor

Mike May

Data Management and Proofreading

Jane Nolting-May

Quality Inspection

Dr Nunu Blue Moon

August 2018

Published by
The Society of Antique Modellers Chapter 35
15 Brit View Road, West Bay, DT6 4HY

First Published 2018
Copyright © The Society of Antique Modellers
Chapter 35 (SAM35)

ISBN Number: 978-0-9572463-1-7

Printed and bound in Great Britain by Creeds Design & Print Ltd,
9c Corbin Way, Gore Cross Business Park, Bridport, Dorset DT6 3UX

Acknowledgements:

The editor gratefully acknowledges the help and assistance freely given by so many people in the production of this book. Unless otherwise stated the photographs are the work of the author of the individual article

Front Cover Photograph: Voetsak tail-chase under threatening skies at Old Warden
Title Page Photograph: Scrutineering can be challenging work!
Rear Cover Photograph: SAM35 members on a summer's day C/L session at their local club field near Bridport – can you identify all those models?
Team Photograph, p.183: Dr W. Walker

SAM35 Membership

If you enjoy reading this Yearbook but are not yet a member of the Society, perhaps you would like to join us. It's very easy - just go to www.sam35.org.uk and click on the membership link. This will provide you with all the information that you need to become a fully-fledged member and enjoy the benefits of our wonderful monthly magazine 'SAM35 Speaks'. If you're unable to access the internet, please call our Membership Secretary Kevin Richards on 01609-772818 or email him at: kevin.richards2@tiscali.co.uk - he will be delighted to receive your enquiry and arrange your membership!

SAM35 Contacts

At the time that this Yearbook was compiled (August 2018), the SAM35 Elected Officers and their contact details were as follows:

Role	Name	Telephone	Email
President	Brian Lever	01733 252416	blever@btinternet.com
Chairman	Ian Lever	01706 875875	ian.lever@ntlworld.com
Secretary	Andrew Housden	01664 480495	andrewhousden@sky.com
Treasurer & Membership	Kevin Richards	01609 772818	kevin.richards2@tiscali.co.uk
F/F Secretary	John Ashmole	01406 370188	editor@peterboroughmfc.org
R/C Secretary	Bill Longley	01258 488833	tasuma@btconnect.com
C/L Secretary	Mike May	07786 034157	bellcrank@witw.org.uk
Public Relations	Roger Brown	01604 890925	robart1@btinternet.com

SAM35 PLANS SERVICE

Plans can be ordered from: Derick Scott Plans Service: www.model-plans.co.uk

Yearbook 16 Virtual Aero-jumble - please help yourself!

TABLE of CONTENTS

Vintage stunter – but guess which one, and what engine?

SAM35 YEARBOOK 16: CLEARED FOR TAKE-OFF!

(Unfortunately, your Editor is unavailable at the moment because he's too busy implementing the new tool control system I've just set up in his workshop. In his absence, he asked me to meet and greet you, our readers, and to make sure you're briefed on what to expect before take-off. I'm very pleased to do so, and will of course make a much better job of it than he would!)

"Ladies and Gentlemen, this is the Quality Inspector speaking... welcome aboard!

"This SAM35 Yearbook is now ready for take-off on your pre-booked pleasure flight around the magical world of classic and vintage aeromodelling. There will be stop-overs at many of your favourite destinations, as well as some exciting and innovative mystery tours intended to open up new horizons for our frequent fliers. We've tried to provide a mixture of the interesting, instructive and possibly infuriating, but always with the aim of keeping you entertained – we do hope that we've succeeded...

"So now, please ensure that your front doors are securely fastened, your mobile telephones are set to automatic, your electronic entertainment equipment is switched on, model-making tools are securely stowed and locked in your sheds, and your tables are fastened in the 'down' position to allow full and free access to drinks and snacks of your choice, then sit back and enjoy this experience – you've earned it!

"Towards the end of your flight, please take a little time to read the Landing Card for an insight into what went on behind the planning of this excursion: you might also like to join with my Editorial team in sincerely thanking our contributors, without whom this venture could never have got off the ground!

HAPPY LANDINGS!

THE QUALITY INSPECTOR

CONFESSIONS OF A CONTEST DIRECTOR
(by John Ashmole)

"Another thirty miles to go; the rainwater that had soaked shoes, socks, trousers and much more during the day was now beginning to pool in the footwell. With the heating turned right up, the inside of the car had become that kind of steam bath in which you still feel cold - and this was meant to be 'our' day, the third day of the Barkston Nationals, with good entries on paper at least for the SAM35 events..."

So what had happened? The Sunday had been the perfect aeromodelling day: a classic Bowden followed by ideal conditions for F/F Scale, but then the rain had come, worsening as the day progressed. "Barkston always gets better in the afternoons" I had advised, wrongly. "It's usually photos of soggy models at the prize-giving but, more importantly, happy smiles". Perhaps they were just relieved that it was all over, but I like to think that our love of the sport will always overcome a few drops of rain!

For some reason, it's always the journeys home that I remember the most. The identities of the winners hardly matter; it's the contentment of the participants that's the overwhelming issue: that, and the dampness of my socks. Contest Directors are a strange breed. Despite all evidence to the contrary, when planning a new event an image of warm sun, calm air and a field strewn with happy modellers always comes to mind! In practice, however, it's sometimes an achievement to force some kind of contest out of a blustery, soaking climate quite unsuitable for any kind of model flying.

At the very first SAM35 event at Buckminster, arranged specifically to draw attention to the new National Flying Centre and to make use of its excellent facilities, the second day began with winds over 20mph and included those squally moments when all and sundry have to scamper to their cars for shelter, but looking across the field at ten in the morning from the comfort of Brian Lever's hospitable caravan, there in the distance was the signature red windcheater of Ken Bates. Oh, no! The CleeMAC crowd is here, there's no getting away with it now; the contests must go ahead, and so they did! For me, it was the day that Hi-Start Glider grew up with spectacular heights from stretched lines singing in the wind, followed by either a big flight and a long walk or... splatt!!

As I drove from Barkston on that other evening in May '17, I began to wonder just why I was doing all this. I love the job, without a doubt, and am deriving great satisfaction from doing it, but did I really know what it would involve when, two years before, I'd been asked to fill in as CD at a previous Nationals? How did it start? Who's really to blame?

"I remember that some years ago, Phil Ball asked me to take over the control table at the "Grantham Grand Prix" briefly while he went away to deal with another matter. Within a few minutes, three FAI Power jobs screamed spectacularly skywards, always an impressive sight, and I remember most of all the proud feeling that I was in some way responsible for them. It was a perfect day with the cream of the country's fliers there in intense competition; I actually felt quite sorry (as well as a bit relieved) when Phil returned!"

'The Future of Free Flight' Conference

It was shortly after the Conference on the Future of Free Flight in 2016 - no, I didn't attend, but I read reports – that I put my initial feelings of depression behind me and decided that something had to be done. At the conference it had been asserted that Free Flight in the UK is in crisis, with only two locations where high performance international class models can be given their head. Venues for Area Centralised contests are few and getting farther between. The escape of models from the field on which their use is authorised is becoming an issue. Ideas for solutions were put forward and either accepted with reluctance, rejected or proved unworkable.

Well, I can offer no help there, but I did feel that the problems that concerned that meeting did not affect the majority of sports flyers, nor those whom my Peterborough MFC club mate and BMFA secretary Mark Benns refers to as 'Sports Contest' flyers, which I take to mean those of us for whom smaller-scale contests provide a structure for our flying but who do not wish to make the huge commitment to fitness, design, trimming, building (or purchasing) that is now often necessary for national or international success.

After some attempts at contest flying in the seventies I'd been away from free flight for many years, building scale fishing boats instead, but was then lured back into the sky and tried thermal soaring for a while before settling into the comfort zone of radio control vintage - the odd 36" hi-start glider was my only venture into free flight. Now a new challenge presented itself: to promote the kind of F/F contest scene that I had left years before.

I spent a year just making up my mind about taking on the role of Free Flight Secretary, coming to my decision after running a soaking and windy Masefield Trophy contest at Old Warden on a day upon which 'my' competitors were the only people to fly F/F. I can remember my good (but sadly late) friend Bernie Nichols standing in full waterproofs in the middle of the flying area, windswept and all alone, just in case somebody wanted a timekeeper – that's dedication! By the time we had finished, and repaired to the hangars for the prize-giving all the tents had been taken down and there were hardly twenty cars left on the field. This was followed by another damp, soggy-socks journey home - I should have learned! But I knew that somehow the show must go on...

By some devious means, my Peterborough club mates had already 'volunteered' me to spend a day acting as joint contest director for the third day of the Nationals. I'm not sure that I was of much use, but ten hours stuck in a lorry with Mike Woodhouse and the Free Flight Technical Committee team was very revealing of the huge amount of time and work needed to make that event go ahead successfully. My respect for their combined efforts grew, while I was also able to make contact again with flying colleagues from the past. Around this time I also found myself acting as CD for the Peterborough Club events as well, so the parts of the jigsaw were falling into place.

Peterborough Club contests epitomize small field flying. The 'Flying Aces' event takes place a week after the Power Nationals in a neighbouring field, which is surrounded by trees and lakes and also boasts a café, car park and caravan site beyond – yes, it's quite a demanding location for a F/F event! On a calmish day the max may be set at 50 seconds, so it's necessary to chose categories of model to suit. This, by the way, exemplifies my 'First Rule of Contest Direction' which is: **"First, Look at the Field."**

Cloud Tramps, which in average hands should be good for at least 50 seconds, have recently been added to the mix of 36" Hi-Start Gliders, Catapult Gliders, and P20 class rubber models such as the 'Sweet Pea'. The latter, however, can out-fly this field unless fitted with an accurate dethermaliser, which has meant the imposition of a minimum weight of 32 grammes (less motor) to encourage the use of something better than a gel timer to get the necessary D/T accuracy. Conventional cabin jobs under 20" can also be entered without limitation, to encourage more participation.

The high performance class 'E20' (initially promoted by the late Ian Middlemiss) is also run, in two classes: one for a specified power-train, and one open to unlimited development. Around 20 members turn up five times a year for these events which begin at four and run until seven in the evening. Even a windy day can calm off dramatically by then, and there have been occasions of furious activity in the final half-hour to record the necessary scores!

On the three dates nearest midsummer, the regular contests are followed by a precision event for the Bernie Nichols Trophy (named after our much-missed Chairman). Competitors ballot for running order and launch cabin jobs in turn to a pre-set target. This happens twice over and can be a beautiful sight, with both vintage and contemporary rubber jobs gently floating away. If you're interested in reading more about these contests, please do click upon the link at www.peterboroughmfc.org/magazines

It only takes a handful of like-minded enthusiasts with similar models and a basic set of agreed rules to make a success of events such as I've described above so why not try it at your club - I'm sure that the editor of 'SAM Speaks' would be willing to print those reports you're going to send in!

Planning a Contest

I firmly believe that if modellers are prepared to take the trouble to design, build and trim their models and then travel to fly them at an event, they must see that their efforts are respected. What's called for is a genuine sporting contest to sensible, agreed rules with a fair outcome. I really don't like the idea of a 'fun event' with a largely random outcome, and I wasn't entirely polite when someone once suggested to me the idea of a 'sealed time' contest in which, if I remember rightly, someone writes down a target time and secretes it in an envelope, everyone flies, and closest to the time is the winner.

I wouldn't insult my models by entering them in such a lottery – as the boy Jack said in 'Lord of the Flies': *"We've got to have rules and obey them!"*

It's a fine balance however, and a CD must listen to competitors to ensure that the published rules are enforced accurately but with due regard to the wishes of all who take part. What matters most? I think the answer is simply that competitors and sports fliers should travel home happy after enjoying a day's structured flying (with the option of a stress-free competitive element for those who want it) and looking forward to doing it all again, with the result secondary to the enjoyment that the day has provided. Whether the models they fly are Cloud Tramps, eight-ounce Wakefields or FAI Power jobs doesn't really matter much to the CD: the basics of running an event remain the same.

Peterborough MFC was asked to prepare a paper on 'Small Field Flying' for the F/F Forum in 2017, for presentation by club chairman Brian Lever. Writing it gave me the opportunity to develop my concept of a modern, relatively low-key small field event.

This was inspired by the part I'd played in the PMFC 'Flying Aces' event, where I looked out across the field and saw, in all directions, small clusters of flyers happily launching, retrieving, chatting and having just the kind of good time that we had intended to provide when planning the event – my goodness, there may even have been ladies sitting around the boundary in deckchairs eating cucumber sandwiches!

To re-state my First Rule of the Contest director, the first consideration in planning has to be the size of the field itself. The extensive menu of possible small field events was carefully chosen so that all classes could be retained within the scope of the space available. Another important consideration was the nature of the participants, which should best be regarded as a group of friends who have come to socialise among like-minded enthusiasts, with just enough competitive edge to add a little spice to the proceedings, although few want long retrieves or too much physical effort. This, of course, applies to most of the SAM 35 'customers' - the days of fitness-training to keep up with large maxes (and to keep our wits sharp until the end of the day - a lost cause for some of us!) are behind us.

Importantly, skills must be properly tested, the best should win most of the time, and there should always be a chance for newcomers or the inexperienced to have occasional success. This must be arranged with due regard to the safety of all concerned, hence the need for two-way radios and a 'retrieval buddy' for those leaving the bounds of an airfield in search of a model.

As for suitable venues, in 2017 the BMFA National Flying Centre at Buckminster became available: invaluable considering the current shortage of good flying sites. For those who can travel that far and perhaps attend the two-day or three-day events put on by the SAM 35 Committee, these offer the experience of 'Mini Nationals' for Vintage, Classic and even contemporary classes of model; I am concerned, however, that not all SAM members and other interested flyers live within easy reach of the East Midlands (*MM: Yes indeed, it **is** a real factor when a venue isn't within day-tripping distance...*)

The idea of 'Area Postal Contests' developed one cold Sunday through a series of shivering, hands-in-pockets conversations between some FFTC stalwarts and myself, and is aimed at encouraging more folk to attend these venues to enjoy flying and mixing with other enthusiasts; an entry of nearly twenty for the P30 'APC' shows that this could be so and that even postal contests, provided that we all play fair with the timings, will develop the kind of inclusivity that I aim for. A person's level of skill hardly matters - it's having a go and being part of an event that is important.

As for those rules: we've all heard of prospective competitors being sent away because their tailfin is covered in the wrong material or for some similar oversight. Such minutiae may have had relevance at a time when many more people were flying: the intention today must be to become as inclusive as possible, within reasonable limits.

Rules today must take due regard of tradition, especially in the Vintage area, but any question regarding acceptance of models, modifications or procedure on the field must take into account the long-term integrity of the class in question and the general wishes of the majority of those who actually turn up and fly. 'Quiet words' and an acceptance of models prepared in the spirit of the rules will go a long way...

But is it all worthwhile?

In front of every silver lining there is always a dark cloud to be found and it isn't necessary to look far to find this one - the gloomy possibility that it's already too late. How many of us are there left? Are there enough potential recruits from radio flyers with a wish to go back to F/F basics, or from the newly retired for whom this is an excellent source of interest, companionship and personal satisfaction? We shouldn't forget either the (relatively few) youngsters who join us, although we have to ask ourselves, why should the average under-30 with his cool RayBans and FPV drone want to spend his time with a lot of grey-haired old men chucking it and chancing it? Maybe that's our Unique Selling Point!

On the positive side, we have available to us decades of designs and advice, good quality kits, adhesives, covering materials, motors, rubber. We can stand with confidence upon the shoulders of those who have gone before. But for me back in 2017, waiting for the post in the days before an Area Postal or Postal event and finding again and again that entries were not coming in it was a depressing experience. Thankfully, the numbers built up as the season went by, culminating in a very good figure for the P30 Postal (second only to the Nationals) and the magnificent response to the "Rubber Bowden" in September which caught me out with insufficient trophies.

At the time of writing (Spring 2018) I await this year's entries with some trepidation, although every effort has been made to establish the SAM 35

Calendar as a menu of events worthy of attention. My friends in the FFTC are very much supportive of my efforts; in fact it has been said in the corridors of power that the future of Free Flight in this country lies with 'our' people.

It is important, however, that this does not remain a one-man-band for much longer. Very happy though I am to continue running events, I may not always be available... and anyway, I shall want to take part as a competitor, which is not always appropriate for a CD. Consequently, I hope that others will join me in running events, will perhaps run comps in other regions sanctioned by SAM 35, and will consequently make a real contribution to the future of our sport.

If you're reading this article in future years, you will be in a position to look back on the Summer of '18 and subsequent seasons and judge for yourselves whether our efforts have borne fruit. As criteria for success, I suggest that if most of the calendar of events that we have initiated is still in place albeit in modified or improved form, and if sufficient fliers are still willing to take part, then this unique and rewarding pursuit is no longer endangered!

Finally, a plea - Contest Directors are not paid, but spend most of their day chained to a desk hoping that everything goes well, or even as I had to do once, clinging like a frightened monkey to the pole of the CD's tent in a Luffenham blizzard while watching other tents and umbrellas go rolling into oblivion across the field...

There is one way in which all those who've enjoyed the day can provide some 'payback' - stay for the prize-giving! Be there. Please! When in the seventies I tried to be a contest flyer, I would often go home in despondency after failing to make a fly-off and not give a thought to the person who had made the day possible.

Those prize-givings that I did attend were sometimes quite emotional events. After a nine-hour day, a gaggle of tired, satisfied, even-scruffier-than-usual free-flighters would assemble with a grudging mutual respect for each others' efforts. We had, after all, spent the day in fairly intense competition with each other and now we came together to applaud the victors and tell of our adventures - this sense of togetherness is valuable both for the contestants and, of course, their CD!

What every CD wants to see - happy competitors!

Arthur Burch - a Unique Life in Aeromodelling
(by Brian D. Jones)

Last autumn I visited Wiltshire to collect a 1950s A/2 glider (Tadpole) that was being donated by the designer/builder, Arthur Burch. Arthur is now 87, and long past chasing F/F models. That afternoon was one of the most memorable I've experienced in recent times, as he shared his aeromodelling experiences and his RAF career *(MM: Brian's article about Arthur's RAF service appears later in this Yearbook)*

Arthur's glider preceded E. Law's early 1950's design of the same name published by Aeromodeller. We did wonder whether the Aeromodeller had 'borrowed' the name for its own 1952 plan, as the Mk 1 version of Arthur's design does seem to pre-date it. Arthur used his design to win the RAF Model Aircraft Association 1952 glider competition, and it still looks very competitive today for the SAM/BMFA vintage glider class.

Arthur's model is beautifully built, with no hint of warps, notwithstanding that it is now 65 years old and hasn't been flown for 45 years! I enjoyed dealing with the inevitable 'hangar rash' over the following winter months and was able to return it to its former glory, as shown in the accompanying picture of me with the Tadpole on an unusually sunny day on Bodmin Moor!

1: Arthur Burch's 'Tadpole' A/2, with its new keeper, Brian Jones

Arthur was a prolific F/F model designer, but his primary interest in the early 1950s was actually control line - he was responsible for the 'Demon King' in 1950, and in 1951 for both 'Lil Toot' and the miniscule 15" biplane 'Lil Abner' (powered by an Elfin .5), and he also won the 1951 RAFMAA C/L scale competition with his own-design FW 190.

If you look through the plans catalogues of the early 1950s for both Aeromodeller and Model Aircraft, you will see his name appearing frequently. One of his charming designs was 'Chug Buggy', a 24" high-wing F/F cabin sport model for the Albon Bambi.

Given the current paucity of really small diesels in the market *(MM: other than those* *in the excellent **Redfin** range, of course!*) this would seem to be an ideal candidate for an electric conversion, so why not build one to fly for yourself? The plan first appeared in Model Aircraft in June 1954 – the accompanying article gave the following advice:

"Our Chug Buggy was built with fairly carefully selected wood to keep the weight down consistent with a strong structure, and the all-up weight, including a full tank, was under 3oz.This was not difficult to achieve and a further reduction in weight could be made by using Wakefield materials. Chug Buggy is best flown with a left climb and glide, which can be adjusted with the aid of a trim tab on the tail fin. The choice of propeller is somewhat critical on an engine of this size and several props of both wood and metal were tried..."

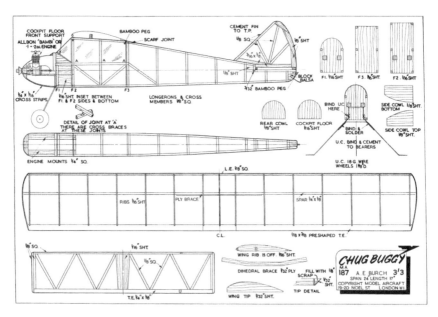

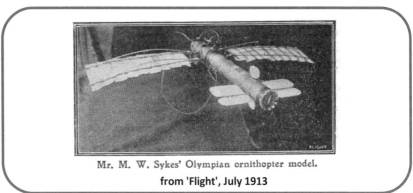

Mr. M. W. Sykes' Olympian ornithopter model.

from 'Flight', July 1913

HOW AEROMODELLING CHANGED MY LIFE *(by Roger May)*

In the January 2016 "SAM Speaks" Colin Hutchinson described a visit he made to the Farnborough wind tunnel, now defunct. I was sent to visit this wind tunnel too as a member of a party of engineers from De Havilland Aircraft Company (DH) of Hatfield. This was back in the early 'fifties when DH was investigating the feasibility of adding suction on upper wing surfaces. This was to increase stalling angles way above normal by preventing or delaying the wing's laminar flow becoming turbulent and breaking up. I'll continue the story of my own wind-tunnel visit after I've explained how aeromodelling led me there!

I'm now 84, and was born in 1934 just before the Aeromodeller magazine was first published. My very first memory of model aircraft was when I was about three - I have a vague impression of a fuselage shaped like an elongated rowing-boat, wings with a wire outline, covered in oiled silk – it would have been a very archaic design even then!

Moving forward to the war years, one Christmas (1943 I think) my father obtained an Astral kit for the Bell Airacobra (a Harry Towner design). The plan was printed on red paper - I was completely fascinated by this and studied it for hours! The wood in the kit wasn't balsa, so my father and I fret-sawed out all the parts and eventually built it into a nice model. It never flew, as the rubber supplied was stripped from old bungee - need I say more! Many years later Alex Imrie, in one of his articles in a 1990s Aeromodeller, described this kit with the red plan and awful wood, and yes, the memories came flooding back. As I was living very near to Alex I visited him and he very kindly gave me a copy of the plan, from which I built my second version of the Airacobra, but from balsa this time!

1: My second Airacobra

By 1945 I was totally smitten with the aeromodelling bug and began building numerous kit models in the company of two other lads that lived in my village. We started to read the 'Aeromodeller', thus gradually gaining the knowledge and skill to trim and fly our planes. After much trial and error I at last had a very satisfactory flight with a Keil Kraft Competitor, and immediately decided that there would be no more kits from now, only our own designs; as I'd become a fan of Mick Farthing I built lightweight rubber jobs in his style. My pals and I decided to join the St Albans club, which had its flying field and meeting place at Nomansland Common.

2: Nomansland Common

(MM: I never knew that Roger's flying field was such an interesting place! It's near Harpenden in Hertfordshire and still hosts model aircraft flying today, besides which it's notorious as the scene of several murders, a venue for bare-knuckle and cock-fighting back in the day, for being the birthplace of steeple-chasing in the UK and as the stamping ground of a famous highwaywoman, the Wicked Lady – what a great name for a F/F model that would be! Now, back to Roger...)

One day I particularly remember saw the three of us cycling to the Common; I was carrying my latest lightweight rubber model on which the dope had blushed badly as the weather was misty and damp. The first person I met was the great George ('Dixielander') Fuller, who cast an expert eye over my effort - I can't remember exactly what he said, but I'm sure it must have been encouraging as he was such a gentleman!

(MM: Dave Hipperson, in his valediction for George Fuller in January 2013, wrote that their long-standing friendship started rather less auspiciously at Chobham Common – "I clearly remember now even 50 years later, on my first ever visit there seeing one of George's Dixielanders climbing into the clear blue sky in front of me as I wheeled my box of very much lesser creations towards his launch point. He wasn't to be trifled with of course. No upstart like me would expect to have much contact with such a star. I can't remember when we first spoke but I am sure it was a put down to keep me in my place and quite right too. We didn't know each other that much in those early days but we were to get on well later on!)

The St Albans club was very active in the early fifties; the 'All-Herts' rallies drew in thousands of people, both modellers and locals, and it was to my genuine surprise that I won the local championship in 1950, mainly because I entered most categories! The club used to hire a coach to go to the main events such as the Northern Heights Gala, where I saw the first outing of Laurie Barr's 'Pinocchio', and Marcus's 'Bazooka', and the weather always seemed to be really fantastic at all the events we attended.

We three also used to cycle the 30-plus miles to Fairlop with a cardboard coffin full of models on our backs. One incident there amused me no end; I was walking in the company of Ron Warring, LG Temple and his daughter as we were following Ron's rubber model (it must have been very calm as we were right underneath it). The model was gliding in a nice circle, but then for some reason, devilment maybe, I said: "Now just watch it spin in!" and lo and behold, It did exactly that! The glare from Ron's face could have killed, but what an extraordinary thing to happen! To be truthful, Ron's model did have a tendency to spin in, as indeed did Norman Marcus's 'Bazooka'…

In 1950 I applied to de Havilland for an apprenticeship; I took a 'Sporty' wing and the plan that I'd built it from, scaled up from an article in the Aeromodeller, and I'm sure that my aircraft knowledge gleaned through aeromodelling helped tremendously in my being successful. When I started at the DH technical school in 1950 I met many old friends from the St Albans club, particularly Bruce Rowe, a fellow rubber enthusiast, who in later years went on to fly for England in the Wakefield Cup - his models were always beautifully built and immaculately finished.

Another member of the St Albans club working at DH was Pete Wright who held a world record in speed with his ED 246 powered model. I can't remember exactly where he worked in DH but it was probably in the offices. He brought his new design of speed model wing in to me in the experimental department. It was made from thin sheet aluminium folded over the leading edge with a single spar about mid-chord, and needed to be riveted at the trailing edge, so I helped him rivet it up with pure aluminium rivets. So that's the story of how my love of modelling got me into DH's factory and into the experimental department, so now let's get back to my visit to Farnborough!

One day a draftsman came into our department with a proposal to suck air though a wing's metal leading edge, the idea being to delay the break-up of the laminar flow and delay stalling. We were asked to drill thousands of holes in strips of aluminium which could then be formed into a leading edge fronting a plenum chamber so the air could be sucked through. Sounds easy until I explain the holes were to be just three or four thousands of an inch in diameter!

Dormer (the specialist drill bit manufacturers) made some special drills but it was a hopeless task, rather like drilling with hair! In the end the Aerotools department in DH came up with the answer, using hardened rods supported by a drilled block which we pressed (not drilled) very carefully through the 20swg 'Alclad' aluminium. It was still not easy, as we had to work out a method of de-burring the holes in the Alclad, which is an aluminium alloy coated with pure soft aluminium; this soft coat had a tendency to block the tiny holes, but eventually we succeeded.

A wing was constructed from wood and the perforated leading edge was attached - the whole assembly was big, about the size of a Tiger Moth's wing. It was then taken down to the Farnborough wind tunnel and set up in a rig where numerous manometers were connected and the fans were started up. The wing reached a very high angle of attack before stalling, from memory about 40 degrees, so you'd immediately think "Success!" But what the boffins had forgotten was that air is not clean, and the tiny holes soon clogged with dust, and even water caused problems, so that was the end of that project!

I went on to become a licensed aircraft engineer, left DH and went to Leavesden Aerodrome, mainly working on light aircraft, which back in the day were just like big

models really. The most difficult job I had was to completely recover a Dragon Rapide with linen, a lot of sewing and doping. Leavesden was where Eddie Riding was based; there were many pictures of him and his models in the Aeromodeller until his death in a terrible accident in a light aircraft - a great loss. *(MM: Eddie was a very accomplished free-flight scale modeller – the Eddie Riding Trophy has been keenly contested by free-flighters ever since)*

After Leavesden I worked for McAlpine Aviation on executive jets, British Aerospace, Britannia Airways, then self-employed and finally retirement. Aircraft have given me an interesting life full of adventures and amusing incidents, and it all started with model aircraft.

Over the years many of my friends in the St Albans MAC achieved aeromodelling success – for example, Pete Wright featured on the covers of 'Aeromodeller' in July '52 and 'Model Aircraft' in December '52, while others had designs published in the aeromodelling press – here are a few I remember:

- Pete Neate – designer of the 'Hi-Ball', the first pylon model published in Aeromodeller in 1947
- George Fuller – designer of the Dixielander and Zoot-Suit, kitted and built in the hundreds and even honored by our fellow American modellers
- Ted Buxton – designer of the 'Barnstormer' stunt control liner appeared in 'Model Aviation' in 1949, and also the 'Filibuster'
- Bruce Rowe - rubber model designer, flew in the UK Wakefield team

- D J S Edwards - built very large and tail-less gliders - his large glider is on the cover of Aeromodeller in July 1952 and two of my friends are launching
- Tony Young – designer of A2 gliders (alas, he defected to Croydon!)
- C M Milford - Class A team racer, designed the 'Black Chiffon', which appeared in the Aeromodeller in October 1952
- Mike Burrows - A2 glider designer, who went on to design carbon bicycles. Although Mike

was originally ignored by all the cycle manufacturers, he was eventually backed by some motor racing companies, and his designs are probably the reason why the UK has done so well in the Olympics. A TV program was made recently about Mike which was used by college lecturers to emphasize how big business often gets it wrong when offered the chance to take on new technology, being risk-averse – other examples include the bagless vacuum cleaner (which made Mr. Dyson a zillionaire!)

Chobham mid-sixties (photo by J O'Donnell) - my most winning open rubber model

19

EARLY AEROMODELLING IN ONTARIO, CANADA
AND THE 'MORGAN SPIRIT' (by Dave Owen)

By the late 1930's, Toronto had emerged as a hotbed of competitive model flying. An air-minded era, monthly magazines, modelling clubs, dedicated individuals and regular competitions all contributed to the awakening of a general interest in aeromodelling in this part of Ontario.

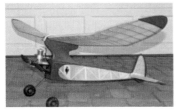

Three men in particular stand out - Fred Bower (who came very close to beating Dick Korda in the 1939 Wakefield Cup competition), Bob Milligan (designer of the gas-powered 'Wasp' - still kitted today – who was also Senior Canadian National Champion of 1938/9), and Roy Nelder (winner of both the 1938 and 1940 Moffett Trophy at the American Nationals); Roy is still thought by many to be the greatest Canadian competitor of his day.

1: Bob Milligan's 'Wasp'

These three were close friends, and practice-flew regularly at Armour Heights; this was a large area that had served as a training centre for the Royal Flying Corps during the First World War and subsequently became the flying-site for the Toronto Flying Club and, for some years, the location of the Canadian Nationals.

The original 'Easy Built Model Aeroplane Company' (established in Toronto in 1932) and its chief Canadian rival, 'Ontario Model Craft', were just the apex of a predictable response to an emerging market. Despite all this activity, it's surprising that, to the best of the writer's knowledge, no Canadian living in Toronto appears to have won the annual Canadian Wakefield competition until well into the 1940s.

The south-western city of Windsor produced several Canadian Wakefield winners between the late 1930s and the early 1950s. At the heart of this success was the Windsor club, which originally met at the municipal YMCA. It had access to the local airport and regularly hosted media-supported competitions, which were so heavily attended that the police reportedly had to attend to keep hordes of spectators at a reasonable distance from the action!

The fact that the large American city of Detroit lay just across the Ambassador Bridge undoubtedly had a very significant positive impact upon the Windsor club members too, with much evidence of cross-border club competitions, to say nothing of the undoubted 'halo effect' that the American Nationals held in the nearby Detroit area had in making Windsor a key hub for Ontario's aeromodelling activity.

So who took up the challenge of supplying modeling goods to Windsor's enthusiasts? Lavalle Walter, winner of the Canadian Wakefield in 1938, 1941 and 1952 seems to have been the first to rise to prominence, despite being half a generation older than most of his fellow club members. He was definitely operating an aeromodelling supply business from his home by the mid-1930's, but we don't know how long this continued after he married and obtained permanent employment towards the end of the Great Depression - quite possibly he may have decided to concentrate exclusively on competition rather than continuing as a supplier.

What is certain is that his enlistment in the wartime RCAF, where he trained as a navigator and later crewed Lysanders on clandestine SOE flights into Occupied Europe, effectively removed him from aeromodelling until the post-war era. Very appropriately, the modern Easy Built model catalogue includes a 'Dime Scale' model of a Lysander – this one was built by Mr Okada in 2010, picture courtesy of the Easy Built Model Company.

2: Dime-Scale Lysander

In 1949 Lavalle was instrumental in forming the Model Aeronautics Association of Canada, and he is also known to have released several kits of his own design and manufacture around this time for local modelers, purely on a hobby basis.

The second major supplier was Richard Morgan. Although he was a decade younger than Lavalle Walter, Richard was a close club friend and had been involved heavily in the hobby for some years before he won the Canadian Wakefield in 1939. Both Lavalle and Walter were excellent craftsmen, and it's probable that the older Walter was a positive influence upon the younger Morgan's development. Described by his friends as extremely enthusiastic and generous to a fault, Richard added his new business 'Morgan Model Supply', operated from his parents' home in Windsor, to his designing and competing activities.

By 1940 Morgan was sawing balsa, packaging dope and mixing cement, in addition to carrying a large stock of basic supplies; these products were all offered through listings similar to those available from Frank Zaic's contemporary Jasco operation. If Lavalle Walter's supply business was still operating at this point, there must have been a local market large enough for both. However, it may well have been that Morgan took advantage of a sudden lack of local competition as businesses like Lavalle's closed due to their owners enlistment in the armed forces.

It's been impossible to determine how long Richard himself was able to maintain his model supply business. Dynamo that he obviously was, it must have been very hard for him to balance its demands against his skilled trade as a tool and die maker and his part-time printing business, all subject to a great deal of local and cross-border competition. On top of this he continued to design further models, not the least of which were his subsequent Wakefield entries. He placed very highly in the Canadian National Wakefield events in Toronto in both 1940 and 1941, having eventually opted for a diamond-fuselaged design whose wing had an Eiffel 400 aerofoil section, this being a distinct change from the Clark Y which he had long favored. Richard's older brother Harry, also a Windsor club member, thought highly of this rocket-climbing design and decided to develop it even further in the later 1940s but alas, no plans of it have survived.

By 1942, Richard was concentrating on gas models and then began full size flying lessons, before moving to job-rich wartime California. His valued trade skills, combined with his mother's American birth, made such a move fairly easy. Understandably, he is not known to have participated further in aeromodelling. Serving in the war as a US infantry rifleman, he had already been decorated for valor so his early death in 1945 on Okinawa at the age of 24 poignantly underscores not only his bravery but also the continuing impact of an aeromodelling legacy from one so young.

While researching information for an article in SAM 35 Yearbook 12 about Richard, contact was made with former members of the Windsor club which led in turn to a very close aeromodelling friend of his from the later 1930's and early war years. This contact, having inherited what had survived of Richard's aeromodelling effects, quickly proved to be of inestimable value in terms of both technical information and personal memories. Most important amongst these was the actual, original 1939 Canadian Wakefield winner, which had been returned to Richard by Burt Konkle of 'Easy Built' models, who had copied it and subsequently released a kit of it (albeit in a somewhat altered form) around 1940 — amazingly, at the time of writing, it is *still* being kitted by

3: Easy Built 'Wakefield' kit built by Paul Kramosil, courtesy of the Easy Built Model Company

the current 'Easy Built' operation – for details of their current range of kits do log in to their excellent website at https://www.easybuiltmodels.com/index.htm.

The 1940 version is certainly vintage in its own right, and probably something of an improvement on the original, but as earlier kit plans show it is not an exact copy of the 1939 winner, nor was Morgan credited on the plan or kit as the original designer. It's not known if Richard Morgan approved of the changes, or even knew of them prior to the kit's release, but he was, characteristically, not known to have expressed any ill will. In contrast, some of his Windsor club-mates were reportedly quite upset at this omission which lasted for some decades until corrected by the current 'Easy Built' proprietor, Dave Niedzielski.

The plan of the original 1939 Wakefield, drawn from the surviving model, has been published comparatively recently by both SAM 35 in the UK and SAM SPEAKS in the United States. The model itself, and an intact, own-design freewheel 36 inch rubber cabin model that Morgan had fortuitously noted on the wing centre section as having been completed in 1940, provided solid evidence that he had not moved away from Clark Y aerofoils until 1941 or so. This impacted in turn upon the interpretation of an undated, unnamed 25¾ inch wingspan rubber cabin-model plan also found amongst his effects; perhaps inspired by Easy Built's desire to kit his Wakefield, Morgan designed the model over the winter of 1939/40, intending to kit it himself for beginners - he must have sensed at least a local market for such a model.

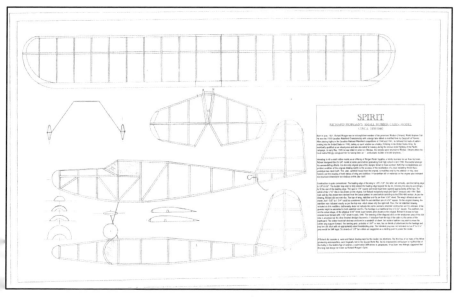

4: Morgan Spirit

For reasons now lost, Morgan did not pursue this further and the plan was not completed in terms of aerofoil and propeller details and there is no recollection of a prototype having been built. Given the intended builder and Morgan's use of Clark Y

sections even at a competitive level at that time, it is reasonable to assume that the now-completed plan would have had a SAM-legal freewheel prop and a flat-bottom section, the latter taken from Clark Y templates that Morgan actually employed. While quite conventional in construction, it's a pretty model both on the ground and in the air, and the plan has had some private

5: Morgan 'Spirit' built by Jim Moseley

circulation after its recent completion, having been entered in at least a few "Two-Bit Plus One" competitions (a North American monetary slang reference to a 26" or less wingspan model!)

It was most fitting that Jim Moseley, well known in vintage aeromodelling circles on both sides of the Atlantic, was probably the first to build, fly and evaluate this previously unknown model by an undeservedly obscure Canadian designer. His comments on what is now often called the 'Morgan Spirit' are most appropriate – he says: "I would speculate that the intention was to design a small model for the sports flyers of the time, a purpose which it would have fulfilled admirably. It's attractive, easy to build and fly, and capable of the magic minute to which novices and younger modellers have always aspired."

Yes, I'm sure Richard Morgan would have been very pleased with that!

[The author wishes to express his gratitude to both the Richard Morgan Estate and Jim Moseley. Without their kind and capable assistance, it would not have been possible to compile this article and present the plan shown above. The Editor also wishes to acknowledge the ownership of the model designs shown in this article by the Easy Built Model Company as the company's own, and the model kit builds and photographs as the kit builders' own]

WORLD DOMINATION BY A TAIL-LESS RUBBER MODEL?

"Be afraid, be very afraid, of THINGS TO COME!" (by Phil M. Buff)

As a prediction of the future from the perspective of 1936, the Alexander Korda film 'Things to Come' (based upon a novel by H. G. Wells) was amazingly accurate in many ways. It's set in an alternative future extending from 1940 to the 1970s, setting a high-tech world organization (no, not the EU!) against a Britain sinking into anarchy under the control of warlords; both sides have forgotten the reasons for going to war, and the world is teetering on the brink of a new Dark Age.

There's a lot of full-sized and model aviation interest in both the story and the cinematography, with the Brits going to war in a motley collection of vintage biplanes salvaged from the WW1 era, while the enemy's air force is well-equipped with streamlined fighters and huge flying-wing bombers. Combat is presented as a mixture of real aircraft vs real aircraft, models against models, and a mix of both - the SFX are very well done.

The hero, Londoner John Cabal, leaves his city job and enrols as a British fighter pilot, flying a biplane to shoot down an enemy monoplane that looks rather like a hapless Mew Gull in defence of the people of London. Eventually, however, he sickens of the war and escapes to found a new political movement called 'Wings over the World' (WOTW – no, not WITW!) based ironically, as we can now see with hindsight, in Iraq. Their organization aims to outlaw war and do away with independent nations, replacing them with a world government of aviating technocrats - I'm sure many SAM35 members would approve!

Cabal then returns to Britain in his new ultra-high-tech fighter to explain the benefits of his new beliefs, but the local warlord captures him and forces him to work making his obsolete biplanes airworthy. It's a bit of a comedown for him, and he soon escapes and returns to Iraq. WOTW eventually wins by putting the populace into a coma using non-lethal gas bombs, then parachuting their troops in to take control, easily enough as the warlord has overdosed on the gas and is dead.

The technocrats take charge, dragging Britain into the future, but this generates opposition from artists and workers who see nothing in it for them. This leads to a rebellion with a mob bent upon wrecking an up-coming moon-shot (using a space-capsule launched by a gun eerily similar in concept, if not scale, to the super-guns allegedly supplied in kit form by UK firms to Saddam Hussein for launching his non-existent WMD missiles from, yes, Iraq!).

Transporting the astronauts in the nick of time to the space-gun using a very Gucci little helicopter, the technocrats manage to blast them off to the moon with Cabal's great-grand-daughter on board, sensibly clad in miniskirt and silk toga. As the space capsule dwindles away into the sky, her father Oswald delivers a stirring speech ("the galaxy or not?") to his pal about what the future might hold for mankind; cue glittering starscape, heavenly choir bawling "Which Shall It Be?" and … roll credits!

Now, you may still be wondering how this visionary film, with its disturbingly accurate predictions of the future, could improve your aeromodelling. Well, as the Quality Inspector has already pointed out, aviation (both model- and full-sized) plays a key role in the plot, with the Warlord's rag-tag gaggle of antique biplanes pitched against that aerial fleet of huge high-tech flying wings (with promenade decks)! In an age long before CGI, the 1930s SFX guys managed to generate convincing footage of models blended with real aircraft to give an impression of massive airforces pitched against each other; when you add in some very good air-to-air combat shots and a full-sized taxi-able mock-up of John

Cabal's super-sleek fighter, it's hard not to be impressed.

The film certainly captured the imagination of British magazines such as the Model Aeroplane Constructor, which was on the bandwagon for the film's launch; the April 1937 cover proudly displays a duo-tone picture of Cabal's iconic tail-less fighter and (best of all) provides a full-sized plan and building instructions inside. This allowed both sci-fi addicts and ordinary aeromodellers to construct their own rubber-powered model fighter by un-stapling the pages and tiling them together to make a full-sized plan, much the same as we do today when we download plans from the internet!

As for the actors in the film, I can remember seeing Raymond Massey, who played John Cabal, in his most famous role as Dr Gillespie in American TV's 'Doctor Kildare' back in 1961, the godfather to every subsequent hospital drama in the world; yes, I really am that old!

Finally, to complete your 'Things to Come' experience, you'll find the plan for Cabal's fighter below, digitally reconstructed from the pages of MAC – we would really love to see one at Old Warden, perhaps as a Cabal-enezer!

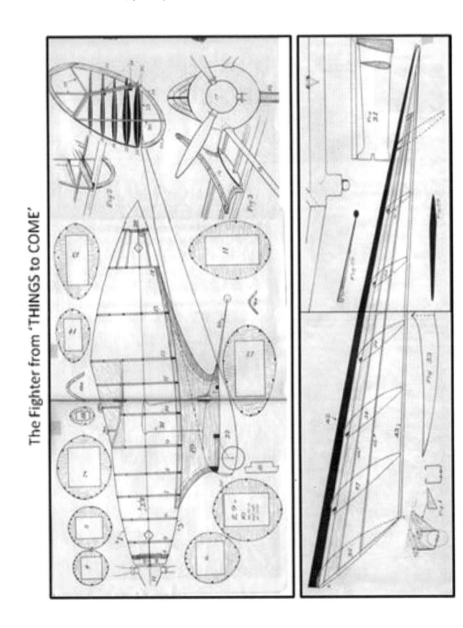

The Fighter from 'THINGS to COME'

Single Channel Spot-Landing Competitions
(by Andy Brough)

I suppose the origin of the Rudder-Only radio competitions we now fly at all the Old Warden meetings can be traced back to a discussion at Vic Smeed's house in 2011. We 'Power Strugglers' were chatting to Vic and he was telling us about the spot-landing competitions he used to run at Old Warden in the early days. This consisted of him going downwind with an umbrella and sticking it in the grass as a target - competitors had to land as close as possible to the umbrella. The models were of course Free Flight, but he wasn't sure of the power units that were being used; certainly they weren't electric but rubber may have been allowed. Mike Parker and I were very interested; why? Because we'd tried for many years to organize competitions for small models at Old Warden without any real success, but here was an idea that could really work well.

Coincidentally, a letter from Vic was later found in a 'Model Aircraft' magazine from way back in June 1949, setting out in detail his proposed rules for spot landing competitions; these were very similar to the basic concept he'd outlined to us more than 60 years later! His rules included a fixed target, a limited motor run, and scoring based upon distance from the target divided by a model's power/glide ratio to provide an effective handicapping system that allowed sports and contest models to compete on equal terms. This must have been the inspiration for Vic's Free Flight umbrella activities at the Old Warden meetings!

1: Enthusiastic spectators following a competitor, note Doug Wass pointing out the model to me!

In 2012 I was still on my crusade to persuade the many powers-that-be to accept the idea that free-flight models could also be flown with the careful use of radio control to keep them within the flying field, but the real game-changer had come the year before when the BMFA published its 'Radio Assisted Free Flight' guidelines This gave event organizers the confidence that there was a structure and a set of rules that had been thought through, was backed by the BMFA, and most importantly meant that this type of flying would be covered by the BMFA's model flyers' insurance scheme. All that was needed was someone to bite the bullet and let us try free-flight and radio-assisted flying together, and that someone turned out to be Ken Sheppard, who ran the Old Warden meetings.

After Vic Smeed's passing, SAM35 organized several events in his memory at the 2012 September Festival of Flight at Old Warden. This initiative resulted in a decision to do two things - produce a trophy, and run a competition. Doug Wass had the trophy made, incorporating Vic's original SMAE badge as well as his facsimile signature. Mike Parker suggested that Vic's spot landing competition might also be an appropriate competition, but it was clear from the start that it

2: The famous Magna going from rarely-seen to prolific with dozens flying at Old Warden

would not be feasible to run it as a free-flight event on a small site like Old Warden, so Doug suggested single-channel radio-assist instead. Doug therefore drafted a set of rules in consultation with Mike Parker and myself; these included a minimum engine run because Doug wanted to prevent anyone from just flying up, around and down, although In the light of experience we've found that it's more difficult to get anywhere near the target from low level. We limited the size of models to something that a Mills .75 could handle, and of course, an umbrella was to be used to mark the landing spot!

So, on the 9th September 2012 the very first single-channel spot-landing competition took place close to the control tower at Old Warden with none other than Ken Sheppard himself on the PA giving a commentary on every flight. The original minimum engine run in the air on that day was planned to be 45 seconds but the bracing breeze forced us to reduce this to 30 seconds, a limit that that we've continued with ever since.

There was no time-limit for completing the landing, just a test of skill to get as close to the umbrella as possible. We had about six entries which was a good start, and with Ken on the microphone drumming up support we soon had a crowd of spectators. It turned out to be a really difficult test as the models would achieve quite a height on a 30 second-plus engine run, but with the wind strength it was a challenge to get back to the umbrella - you let the model go down-wind at your peril!

Chris Giles triumphed at that first event with the inevitable 'Tomboy' and won a Vic Smeed 'Chatterbox' as a prize, which he intended to enter the following year.

Following this success I then had further discussions with Ken Sheppard and he agreed that we could run another competition at the Old Warden Mayfly meeting to complement the now-to-be annual Vic Smeed memorial event in September.

Things moved further forward in 2012; I was with Doug Wass when he spotted a reasonably-priced NOS Magna kit which, after some haggling, he bought at a reasonable price. It turned out that this design had been his first power model, just as it had been mine, so for old times' sake he decided not to build it but to use it as a template for the production of new Magna kits, which was duly achieved that winter. It was then a logical step to nominate this design for the upcoming Mayfly spot-landing event.

3: Brian Jenkins launching his Magna in May 2017

This was held in a fresh breeze with clouds threatening rain, but six of us had a go, with the engine run again dropped to 30 seconds. The proceedings were managed by Wesley Denton with marker-sticks used to record the distance of the nose of the model to the umbrella. Once again Ken gave an excellent commentary, Alex Phinn donated an engine for the prize, and Brian Ball won with his Mills powered Magna. It's worth remembering that the Magna can be scaled to any size up or down as long as it meets the 0.8cc and weight limit (500 grams at the time of writing). Doug made a smaller version as a kit and he also entered a larger version. The Magna is a remarkable flyer with good penetration - as I noted on the day: "No-one would have flown a F/F Magna on such a day, but we flew with rudder-only control and landed safely and not too far away!" We also ran this competition again in September.

By 2014 general flying using RTA (radio trimmed/assisted) had become widely accepted and the entry at the Mayfly was a healthy dozen, which far exceeded any power competition we'd ever held at Old Warden before. Dave Kay won with an Irvine Mills-powered model and a home-made transmitter built (as per the golden age of single-channel radio) into an OXO-tin!

4: Doug Wass presenting the Vic Smeed Trophy to Brian Jenkins in September 2014 (Jim Woodside looks on...)

As RTA was now becoming popular at Old Warden, we added another open competition at the Scale Weekend, for which any model meeting our engine and weight limits could be used. Why we didn't specify that it had to be a scale model I really don't know, except it would have required more work from entrants and the numbers would probably have been low as a result. The first of these open spot-landing events was held in great weather on July 20th 2014 with ten entries. A good range of designs took part but a Magna still won, this time flown by Alan Poulton. I achieved my best position ever with third place flying my new 'Lofty Lassie', another Vic Smeed design.

September saw 15 entries in the Vic Smeed spot landing held in glorious weather, although this didn't make hitting the spot easy, far from it! Despite the benign conditions all flyers landed downwind of the spot and even the winner, Brian Jenkins, landed 5.4 metres away - see, no wind to slow the model down.....

5: Doug Wass with his Vic Smeed-designed Damsel

In 2016 Doug Wass introduced the spot-landing league with a trophy for the most consistent performer over the three Old Warden meetings. Points are awarded to each contestant by dividing their distance from the umbrella by the winner's distance – the competitor with the fewest points over the three meetings is the champion. Weather plays an important part and the winner could actually be a long way from the spot but awarding points based the winner's distance seems to work well, and of course you can win the league and never win a competition! The first trophy-winner was Toby Collis, appearing on the cover of the SAM35 'Speaks' in December 2016, and to prove it was no fluke he also won the league in 2017!

Spot-landing competitions are now firmly part of the Old Warden weekends, with the faithful gathering to test their luck, nerve and skill in front of an appreciative crowd who always enjoy watching the fun. Looking back from the 2018 Mayfly, we've now run 16 competitions at Old Warden, as well as events at the Free Flight Nationals, and we are also planning to hold additional competitions at the BMFA's new model flying site at Buckminster. So what have we learned from running these events?

FIrstly, don't let your model go too far downwind – if you do, you'll never get it back to the marker!

Secondly, although downwind landings look achievable, you'll go straight past the umbrella unless you're very lucky.

Thirdly, having no elevator control makes the whole exercise much more difficult - whilst watching the model itself you somehow have to position it over the spot, predict the wind speed and gauge the right approach direction as you constantly lose height. Lastly, as well as a skill requirement there's also a luck element that's a great leveller, rather like the Bowden; this is what makes it open to all and a great spectator sport!

If you fancy taking part you'll need a Magna for the Mayfly, any model for the Scale Weekend and a Vic Smeed model for the Festival of Flight, whilst our other venues allow any model up to Junior 60 size, but in all cases please do remember to disable the elevator and throttle controls if they're fitted. There are other events such as the precision competitions at Buckminster and the Nationals which are similar to our spot-landing challenge, but which allow models fitted with an elevator to use it, although they do impose a two-minute target time to land in a marked area - see the SAM35 website for more details.

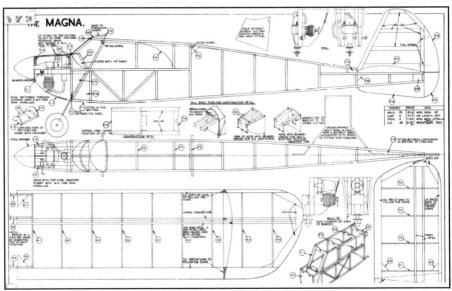

Mercury Magna Plan courtesy of www.outerzone.co.uk/plan_details.asp?ID=4811

COUSIN LEWIS – A GLIDING CONVERT!
(by Gordon 'Gamma' Rae)

At about ten years of age I made a regular Sunday morning pilgrimage with my uncle Maurice to the large Victorian house where the May family lived. We spent all our time in Lewis's modelling workshop in the cellar where we would sit and watch Lewis at work on his models. Lewis was a carpenter by trade and an excellent model aircraft builder in his spare time - he was some ten years older than me.

1: Cousin Lewis in his workshop – Big Gee under construction

All his aircraft were scale and invariably built from kits, and mostly biplanes - for instance there was a very fine scale Hawker Audax - I can particularly remember the intricacy with which he constructed the rear cockpit-mounted Lewis gun on its working Scarff ring mount. The first model completed by Lewis was a one-third scale cabin biplane, rubber powered – although it was never actually flown! He constructed a scale hangar on a concrete slab in his back garden to house this large biplane, which to my young eyes was utterly spectacular! After a long lay-off from modelling (including getting married) he started again after seeing my gliding models in 1980. From then on Lewis only constructed model gliders that I'd designed. The majority of our flying was slope soaring off the Malvern Hills, seven miles long north to south with long westerly-facing slopes into the prevailing wind.

We also indulged ourselves with some tow line and bungee-line flat field flying from Fish Meadow near Upon-upon-Severn - all great fun!

2: 'Finger 110' on the Malverns

3: Lewis with Gordon's low-wing Gull slope soarer

The Wacky World of Clan Weird!
(by Colin Hutchinson)

This article was originally intended to be the first of an occasional series about unorthodox models, articles that I hoped to write and fit into 'SAM Speaks' as space permitted, but time went by, the space did not materialise; then Yearbook 16 started to take shape and it seemed to offer a natural home for my Saucery!

I do like unusual models, and over the years have built many. In fact, I went to Salisbury Plain to fly a few weeks ago with several models, and none of them had conventional wings. Some, like the 'Rezenebe' Ebenezer, have proven to be such excellent flyers once trimmed that they became models I flew all the time.

1: Colin's Rezenebe

I recall one occasion at Middle Wallop when flying the Rezenebe, I filled up the Cox 010, launched the model and off it went into the wide blue yonder. A tankful usually got a good flight for the model, but the glide always brought it down within the airfield, and on this occasion it did just that. However, I was unable to keep it in sight all the time as the airfield undulates, and sure enough it disappeared behind a small hillock when it landed.

I wasn't worried by this, and kept walking in the direction I'd last seen it. Then, to my amazement, over the undulation came two flyers, one carrying my Rezenebe, and the other dragging a Boehle Giant, the biggest free flight model I have ever seen, all 14 foot 8 inch span of it! Talk about little and large, it made the Rezenebe look even smaller than usual! This behemoth was designed for pre-war USA Texaco Trophy events by Vernon Boehle, (pronounced Bailey) a Canadian who used a Baby Cyclone Sparkie (.36ci) for power.

2: A Boehle Giant

(MM: the Giant was originally featured in the 1937 Zaic Yearbook – you'll find it recaptured in the Plans Chest here in our own Yearbook 16, a mere 81 years later!)

Getting back to the subject of unorthodox models, (actually I suppose the Giant could be classed as such due to its huge size), I have such a love of them that I've been hailed as 'The Chieftain of Clan Weird' as if there actually is a club or association for funny model builders!

As a pal once said to my Trouble and Strife at Old Warden: "Ah yes, your husband is that strange flyer – er, sorry, I meant that flyer of strange models!" Truth to tell, I don't have as many unorthodox models as I did simply due to wear and tear, but yes, I do still build them!

The Sorcerer

This reasonably well-known model is of course a flying disc, with an S-shaped curve built into the wing to provide lift. It flies well for such a low aspect ratio wing,

3: The Sorcerer

and, if built light, has a surprisingly good glide. I have made at least five versions over the years, with only two being the original size of 18" span. It was designed by John Taylor and published in 'Aeromodeller; rather sadly he was never credited on the plan, but now you all know!

My first rendition flew for many years until diesel fuel soaked so far into the structure that it had to be scrapped. I can't remember any fly-aways, but as the decoration was obtained from my place of work around 25 years ago, my memory might be experiencing software errors. I remember that just after the plan was published several examples could be seen airborne at Epsom Downs, making the sky appear to be full of UFO's - the truth is out there somewhere!

The main difficulty with the design is keeping the 1/16" sheet wing straight. Although the wing is bent into an 'S' shape, there is a tendency for warps to set in. However, I have found that once settled it does not change again.

Another challenge can be locating the model after it has landed, as it has little in the way of vertical surfaces and no undercarriage to tip up the back end on landing; it virtually

4: Vertical Arrival = Easy Retrieval!

disappears even if the grass is short, so a very careful eye has to be kept on it during the flight.

Expanding the Fleet

Last year I built a second full-sized copy to replace the original, and that has now flown many times on Salisbury Plain with the original .5cc Dart for power. I have always been pleasantly surprised by the glide, which, for a very low-aspect ratio wing, is quite flat. Over the years I have also tried several other sizes, some of which have been successful, while others have not.

5: Sorcerer in Flight

The most successful of them is a 13 inch span version that I still have and fly, powered with a Schlosser .25cc diesel – it's at least ten years old and is beginning to show its age! The least successful was a 10 inch version powered with an Arne Hende .25cc Mini Dyno engine that unfortunately proved to be far too pokey for the model. Its high speed made me think that its rather robust arrivals might damage the engine

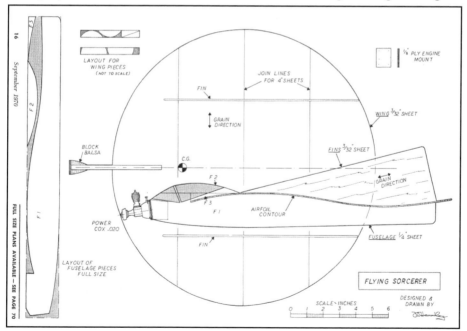

6: Flying Sorcerer

before I managed to get the model trimmed satisfactorily, so I binned it. I then went in the opposite direction and built a 24 inch diameter span version, powered with a DC Sabre.

This also proved to be somewhat over-powered, and made the ground shake when it landed, eventually doing its best to destroy itself landing heavily on Salisbury Plain – alas, it's never been repaired. I have a hankering to try this size again, but might try Depron rather than balsa construction, as Depron will not change shape and is about the same weight. In addition I have a large pot of water-based resin that needs using up, which would, I think, make it proof against diesel fuel.

Finally, I have a vague memory of trying a 6 inch span diameter indoor version, but can't remember what happened to it so I assume it wasn't successful. However, as the saying goes, "Nothing ventured, nothing gained," so I have built another 6 inch version. Power will be provided by a Gasparin G10 CO2 motor – look out for flying reports in 'Speaks'!

UFO Watch!

'Flying Sorceror': There are, of course, many other flying discs and rings that I know about – the next one was designed by Jack Headley; I've seen it at Old Warden and it does seem to fly well. Of course, it is very similar to the Sorcerer (note spelling!) It was described in an article in the American 'Aircraft Modeller' magazine issue 09-70 which asked: "Do you believe in flying saucers? Now you can - this one's for real, an .020-powered free- flighter..."

'Spinning Disc Saucer' - Roy Clough's Spinning Disc Saucer was featured in an article in the 'American Modeler' magazine issue 08-62, which said: "It floats up weirdly with a peculiar ululating whine reminiscent of a flying saucer from a science-fiction movie. Then, moving through the air as gracefully as a gull it begins its descent and returns to earth as gently

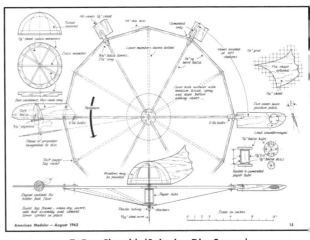

7: Roy Clough's 'Spinning Disc Saucer'

as a feather. This novel plane is sure to stop the show at any flying site..." – yes, very poetic indeed!

'Flatcat': Ernst Skirde's saucer was featured in the 'American Modeler' magazine issue 09-59 which reported:

"Bored with run-of-the-mill models? Here is a simple, unbreakable 'saucer' that can be thrown together within an hour.

"Practically foolproof, it was the sensation of the German Nationals at Kassel back in '59. Instructions are almost unnecessary, if a few basic dimensions are adhered to.

"Primarily, it's a ducted fan, with rotor blades attached to the engine mount..."

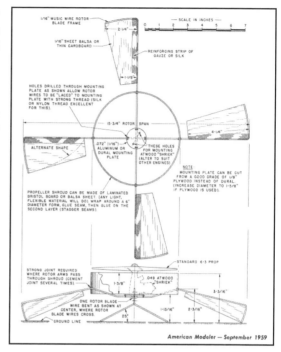

American Modeler — September 1959

Jetex: for you fizzle-fizzle-whoosh enthusiasts, there are at least three Jetex powered flying discs on Roger Simmons' website – follow this link: **http://archivesite.jetex.org/cja/plans-misc.html**

Cox and other Ready-to-Spin Saucers

Over the years there have been many reported sightings of flying saucers all over the world, but we know that they don't exist, don't we? *(MM – hmm, try asking the inhabitants of Roswell that!)* Whatever the official view, I know that I've personally seen three of them, all of them powered by the same out-of-this-world power plant, the Cox 049, and all varying in complexity.

All I can say is I had a lot of fun with them, although I didn't see any little green men! Cox marketed three different saucer designs over the years, and all except the oldest flew well. I suppose you can call it flying, can't you, or should it be powered Frisbee-ing?

My Wandering Whirlygigs

8: Colin's ex-Alan Jupp Spineroo

I bought my ‚Spineroo, (It was built by Alan Jupp) soon after I saw someone flying one at Middle Wallop in the autumn of 2000. I remember one flight particularly well, when the disc started to fly but would not climb because the engine had gone slightly rich. It veered off horizontally towards the rows of parked cars, went between two of them and came out the other side. The engine then leaned out and it started to climb vertically, followed by howls of hysterical laughter from myself and the other observers!

The **Nomad** is the youngest of my flying saucers (manufactured in 1990/2000), and the most sophisticated, but perhaps not as much fun as a result. However, it always attracted a lot of attention because it was unusual. My first attempts produced sniggers from my club-mates because after taking ages to start the engine it then only managed a flight of five seconds, making a ground hop of about three feet!

However, once the engine was run-in I would regularly get flights of up to 250 feet. In windless conditions. it would usually rise vertically then land almost at my feet, but on one occasion at Chobham Common I happened to launch into rising air and it went nearly OOS before returning to earth. On the other hand, in turbulent air it could become unstable and turn itself upside-down, landing on its engine or on the expanded polystyrene frame, the spinning motion causing it to roll in tight circles on the short Middle Wallop grass buzzing like a Raid-sprayed bluebottle! It had one rather delightfully eccentric characteristic that appeared in the auto-rotation phase of the flight - about half way through the descent it would begin to wobble, rather like a buckled bicycle wheel... near the end of its life so much fuel had soaked into the foam that it once took off leaving the foam surround behind, although it still managed to fly in quite a stable manner!

Flying Saucer

I bought this from a chap on eBay, and what with a UK postal strike, and the fact that the post in the seller's country was slow, the Saucer (of 1980-90 vintage) took two months to arrive from the Philippines, complete with several (thankfully deceased) spiders, but it was well worth the wait! Once the engine was run-in it flew as well as the Nomad, rising to a majestic height. It was much less sophisticated than the Nomad, and relied on the engine, contained within a small duct, to provide the lifting power. There was very little weight for it to lift, as it was largely constructed from white expanded polystyrene, so it rose more quickly and fell more slowly than the Nomad, but then the Nomad was several seasons old at the time and its polystyrene surround was rather fuel-soaked.

Rotation in the opposite direction to the propeller provides its stability, and it must be launched by firmly rotating it clockwise. On the first launch I managed to do this anticlockwise instead, so the machine rose, but the rotation began to slow until it stopped and started to spin clockwise. On another occasion, when a friend was trying the photograph it, I'd set the engine a bit rich so it did not climb more than a few feet, but whilst doing so it managed two three circuits around the photographer, much to his amusement!

9: Flying Fruit Bowl

Star Cruiser

This was yet another eBay purchase, this time from a chap in the UK; it's the oldest of my saucers (manufactured around the 1970/80s), and is by far the heaviest

- this one is built from flexible plastic, and weighs more than the two of the others put together.

After several attempts to get it into the air I finally managed a few reasonable flights. The needle valve setting was very critical, and repeated attempts to fly it resulted in flights typically lifting only a few feet, with several landings during each flight, followed by self-launches, and sometimes turnovers with the machine trying to eat grass! When the engine stops with the saucer at a good height, the glide is seriously fast and steep - on occasions it even managed to dig holes in the soft grass on landing!

Conclusion

So as you can see, there are a lot of funny (amusing, strange, downright puzzling!) designs out there – so why not go searching for them on the free plans websites (Outerzone, Aero-Fred, Hip Pocket and others) build something simple to start with and have lots of crazy fun – and in doing so you'll be automatically enrolled in my Clan Weird!

10: Not a Flying Saucer, but certainly another wacky model from Clan Weird!

ULTRA-LOW FLYING - TETHERED CARS!

(by Steve Betney)

The strong links between model aircraft and tethered model cars are very long established. Tethered car activities started in the USA during the 1930s and moved to the UK during World War 2, when powered model aircraft were banned. The 1942

Aeromodeller magazine carried a series of articles including plans for the Galeota AG Midget Car (*MM: see our Plans Chest!),* the "Wasp" airscrew-driven car, and the large Russell SS 100, with a national competition being staged for two classes of car, with engines up to 6cc and engines up to 10cc, all spark ignition of course (glow and diesel power was still to come!)

This eventually led to the formation of the British Model Car Club (BMCC) in the London area in 1944. Most British models were scale or semi-scale with centrifugal clutches, running at 30-50mph speeds on circular tracks, using model aircraft wheels (very difficult to obtain at the time) or ashtray-type scale wheels.

American cars were usually non-scale types designed for much higher maximum speeds than those in the UK, using cast aluminium bodies and direct drive (no clutches) – they required push-starting - and enthusiasts had a good range of suitable tyres, racing engines and other parts readily available even in wartime. After WW2, mass-produced smaller cars by Cox, Wen-Mac and other suppliers became widely available; at the time these cars, with engines

between .049 to .15 cubic inches, were called control-line cars or tether-cars in the US, and were attached by only one tether wire to a handle or fixed central pylon.

In May 1945, the Drysdale Press published D A Russell's 'Model Race Cars' booklet, which included details of the first ten pioneering i/c powered cars, most at around one-eighth full size, with construction plans being made available for seven of these; by June 1946 the BMCC had established its headquarters at the dedicated 72' diameter track at Eaton Bray, and interest really started to grow.

In this early post-WW2 period clubs were being established nationwide, not just in the London area, and dedicated monthly magazines were available. Percival Marshall's 'Model Car News', running from August 1946 until February 1950, was largely just narrative and photographs with a cover price of 6d (2½p). Drysdale's 'Model Cars' running from October 1946 to November 1950 was a better bet for construction details and plans, but at 1s 3d (just over 6p!) must have made a big hole in a younger modeller's pocket money. These publications included advertisements for a plethora of model car parts, plans, kits and suitable engines (albeit model aircraft types - including diesels by now rather than dedicated car power plants - until 1948). By 1947, Tyres and spares were readily available from UK companies such as Hastings 1066, ZN, Dunlop, Replica and many others, while full-size car manufacturers such as Austin and MG sponsored tethered car events & presented trophies

D A Russell and G H Deason's excellent 'Motor Racing in Miniature' book was published by the Drysdale Press in 1947, followed a couple of years later by Deason's 'Model Car Manual', which had more construction drawings and details, by now largely featuring diesel engine power.

Also in 1947, John S Oliver's Battleaxe 2cc diesel appeared, at first in single cylinder aircraft form, but in 1948 in tethered-car twin-shaft configuration with both shafts driven by a common crank, and car development moved into smaller scale models running at higher speeds, along with rail cars

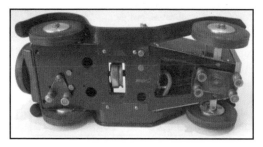

running on a single track guide with 'Zonkers' to guide them. These were usually powered by small diesel engines and became very popular. Oliver Raylite wheels capable of high track speeds came along in 1948 then, in 1950, the world famous Oliver Tiger 2.5cc diesel motor went into production, most commonly in twin-shaft car form at first. John Oliver also introduced tethered car kits during this time of burgeoning interest, but by the mid-1950s the sport had all but faded away as the dedicated circular tracks disappeared one by one, with rail cars falling into a similar decline over a relatively short period.

Today there is only one proper track left in the UK for enthusiasts to run their cars on, built by Peter Hill, Secretary of the Retro Racing Club at his home in Great Carlton in Lincolnshire, and gratefully used by members at RRC at weekend track days.

The roll-call of famous aeromodelling personalities involved in tethered cars is impressive: D A Russell, Phil Smith, Gerry Buck, Ian (Bill) Moore, Ken Proctor, Basil Miles, Vic Smeed, Ken Proctor and Ken Bedford to name but a few. Manufacturers offering cars in kit or complete form included KeilKraft, E D, Veron, Masco, Mercury, Jetex and others. Quite a few current SAM 35 members also belong to the RRC and still indulge in building and running all kinds of tethered cars, but mainly retro types, including Dick Roberts, Jan Huning, George Sayell, John Huntley, John Goodall, Dave Coe, Oliver Monk, Dave Hume, Kevin Richards and myself, so why not come and join in the fun? In addition to the overall attraction of operating control line models that's enjoyed by many SAM35 members, there's a most interesting extra engineering aspect to this hobby which many of us find irresistible, and we hope that many of you will do too.

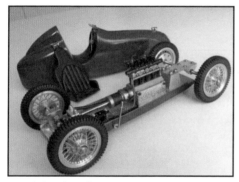

To regain their deserved popularity, tethered cars just need better exposure to attract a larger following and a regular, more public venue at which they can operate; hopefully these articles will provide the necessary exposure, while the good news on a venue is that the RRC is working closely with a very supportive BMFA to ensure that its members will be able to run cars on the planned caged, hard-surface control line circle when this is constructed at Buckminster Lodge.

After reading the 'Diesel Domination' article in this Yearbook, you might like to visit Hugh & Lynn Blowers' excellent resource at their www.onthewire.co.uk website, for comprehensive coverage of both the history and contemporary activities of tethered cars, tethered hydroplanes and rail cars. There is a regular section covering the Retro Racing Club's activities at Great Carlton in the UK with a meeting diary; just contact Peter Hill by email at arty.pole@gmail.com , or any of the SAM members named above for a guest invitation– we're sure that you'll be hooked too!

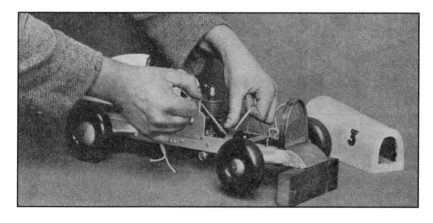

DIESEL DOMINATION!
Tethered Cars and the Olivers *(by Hugh and Lynn Blower)*

Very few manufacturers in the world of modelling have achieved such success and status as the Olivers. Their record in powering tethered cars and model aircraft in combat and team-racing has been second to none, and their name is still held in such high regard that even today, collectors avidly seek out anything related to the output of their company. Paradoxically however, the genesis of the Oliver marque had nothing whatsoever to do with model products, as we shall see.

John Arthur Oliver (JAO) originally worked for Raleigh Cycles in Nottingham before becoming self-employed, repairing motorcycles and light cars during the great economic depression in the 1930s. Through hard work the J A Oliver (Engineering) business survived the turmoil, eventually taking on premises and setting up a cycle shop in Radford Road Nottingham, an address that was to become known worldwide.

Battleaxe Single

While the war years were spent producing parts for the nearby Royal Ordnance Factory, the move into the design and manufacture of model diesel aero-engines came about almost by accident, but this was actually providential as the cycle business had begun to struggle in the immediate post-war period.

John S Oliver and his father had already developed an interest in small model engines, especially the compression ignition type now universally known as 'diesels', which were widely in use on the continent. These were rapidly replacing spark ignition motors, especially in the smaller sizes, and in 1947 this led J A Oliver to start producing parts for his first engine, the 2cc 'Battleaxe', based loosely upon the Swiss 'Dyno' motor.

Battleaxe Twinshaft

It hasn't been possible to establish exactly what prompted JAO to become involved with tethered cars, yet it is certain that he quickly adopted the principle of adding a second drive shaft to the back of the motor, with the wheels attached directly to the shafts, thus creating the 'Twinshaft' motor that would make the company's name. This layout removed the need for the clutches, gearboxes and shafts that were the norm at that time; when the motor was added to a basic chassis, it resulted in a cheap and simple entry into tethered car racing.

John junior joined the company on leaving the RAF, and was soon at work finishing off the second 'Oliver' car - the 'Challenge'. This employed a tubular alloy chassis, piano-wire front suspension and a Twinshaft direct drive Battleaxe motor enlarged to 2.5cc, with bought-in wheels and tyres attached to the drive shafts.

1948 2.5 Twinshaft

In April 1948 JAO was one of the founder members of the Nottingham Club, whose members initially used an indoor track before moving out to Bassingfield in 1951. At their first track day in June, JAO recorded 42.3mph with his number 2 car that had the 2.5cc motor, whilst the number 1 car with the original 2cc motor did 41mph. This signalled the start of the Olivers' racing careers, although these two cars were quickly superseded and retired from the track.

At the Hastings Trophy event held at Eaton Bray, Jack Parker and his ED powered car beat the Olivers' entry by nearly 6mph - the Oliver motor was far from competitive against the EDs as yet, but that was soon to change and by doing so bring their name to the forefront of tethered car racing. At the Meteor Club meeting on October 31st JAO set a new British 2.5cc record of 55.5mph using a 'teardrop' style car and a 9-port development of the Battleaxe motor, with his son finishing third at 41mph with the back-up car. Significantly, the first three 2.5cc cars were faster than any of the 5cc entrants. Noted racer Jack Parker eventually became a customer of the Olivers, although his request for a 'discount' on a car was politely refused!

"Two-Five"

Meanwhile, work was continuing on developing the first commercial Oliver car. This would be somewhat different in design to those the Olivers were using for their own racing; both JA and JS were running teardrop-style cars, one of which was the 'Newt', as well as a more conventional semi-scale type car that would become known as the 'Busy'. The new commercial car was called the Two-Five and was developed from the 'Challenge'. The chassis was now folded aluminium, still with piano-wire torsion front suspension and the nine port motor held onto pan with U-bolts round the shaft housings. Raylite solid tyres now replaced the earlier '1066' items, and were now secured with very large hexagonal tube nuts.

The Olivers had established a commercial tie-in with Raylite, another Nottingham company, allowing Raylite to sell Oliver motors under their own name and Oliver to use Raylite bonded tyres. Advertisements first appeared from both these companies in the December issue of Model Car News in 1948. JA Oliver offered the complete Two-Five chassis with motor, tank and tether brackets at £9-17-6, while the motor alone was £6-19-6 (wheels 18/- extra). Raylite advertised just one size of wheel, claiming that it had been tested to 28,000rpm.

An advertisement appeared in January 1949 showing the complete Two-Five car, although the body was the responsibility of the purchaser. The advertisement in March 1949 changed slightly as it now included endorsements from customers of the engines.

In April a further version of the original motor, now identified as the MkII and called the Jaguar Twinshaft, was announced, on which the most obvious differences were the turned portion of the crankcase below the exhausts and the black anodised finish. The earlier version was still available at the slightly higher price of £7-17-6, although this now included a pair of wheels, while the new motor was priced at £8-18-6. In a magazine test the Jaguar produced just over 0.2bhp at 8,700rpm although Oliver only claimed 0.16. Because of its higher rpm the new motor required smaller tyres, which were advertised by Raylite in May of that year. JSO raced the 'teardrop' car in the MCA eliminators and National final, both held at the Derby track. He won each and every round of the 2.5cc Class, beating all other competitors by a huge margin in the finals.

The birth of the motor that was to become the watchword for performance for the next decade or so was due in no small way to Gerry Buck from nearby Stoke on Trent. Gerry was a multiple record holder in the 10cc Class, but as a reaction to mumblings about his 'superb facilities' being responsible for his success he decided to enter the 2.5cc Class with the very simplest of cars. He bolted a standard 2.49cc Elfin aero-engine to a basic chassis with a driving wheel attached where the prop would normally be, and covered it with an even more basic body.

Within a couple of weeks this 'Wee' car was exceeding 60mph and went on to take British and Open 2.5cc records at every distance up to 1 mile and even set a record for 10 miles.

Meanwhile, JAO had accepted an invitation to travel to Sweden in the autumn as part of the British team, but both he and JSO were well aware of the leap in speed that Gerry Buck had made and realised that their Jaguar was not going to be competitive, either against Gerry or the best the Swedes could muster. As a result, a new engine was designed and built in very short order. The side-port layout was abandoned in favour of a disc valve, there being no time to consider a shaft valve, although finding room for the disc in the Twinshaft layout did cause considerable head-scratching. The solution was to use a cut-out in the slave crank disc as the valve, running on the inner face of the separate shaft housing that also carried the venturi.

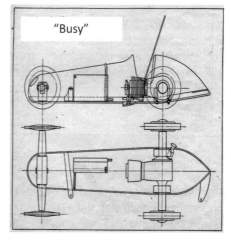

"Busy"

According to John S, the bore and stroke were a 'matter of guesswork' but even so, the motor was built in little over three days, and the only component it shared with the Jaguar was the compression screw. There was no time to build a chassis, so 'Busy' was dug out and the new motor installed. A quick and 'iffy' visit was made to the Derby track to see if the motor worked before JAO, Harry Howlett and the three cars were packed for the trip. At the Stockholm meeting 'Busy' duly won the 2.5cc class at over 64mph with Gerry Buck second nearly 10mph slower. At Orebro the roles were reversed as JA ignored his son's entreaties before he left - 'anything over 63mph DON'T FIDDLE', and was 2mph slower. Gerry meanwhile had twiddled his needle valve and compression screw to almost match the speed JAO's achieved in Stockholm.

So impressed were the Swedish competitors with the Oliver engines that JAO was reputed to have come home with orders for nearly 50 motors. The speed with which the motor was made meant that it was still held onto the chassis by U-bolts round the housings, so the motor was redesigned with a cast crankcase with a flat plate underneath to allow the motor to be bolted straight into a chassis, so establishing the iconic design we know now. This new motor became the RV, although it is understood that only around seven were produced. Not long after their return from Sweden, fellow team-member Alex Snelling from Edmonton requested that a ball raced version be built for him, which became the RVB.

'Busy' formed the basis of the first Oliver car made completely from castings. This was the second design to be called a Two-Five. At the Meteor Club open day in Staffordshire the prizes were being presented by the West Ham and

RV (ex Gerry Buck)

England speedway rider Harold Stevenson (known on the tracks as 'Tiger') and it was at his suggestion that John Oliver called the as-yet unnamed motor the 'Tiger'; in doing so he created a brand known worldwide to this day. The newly-named 'Tiger' RV was then marketed at £7-10-0, and in December the RVB ball-bearing version followed at £8-18-6. Taking the lead from Gerry Buck, a single-ended BR model was also available at £6-15-0, and the Tiger Two-Five car kit was available at £10-9-6.

Tiger Two-Five Chassis

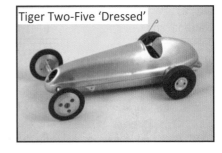

Tiger Two-Five 'Dressed'

In April 1950 the company was advertising ready-built and tested Tiger cars at £14-18-0. Harry Howlett was an integral part of the Oliver operation, being a close friend

The 'Alfa'

and enthusiast, but more importantly the producer of all the castings for the Olivers. Having travelled to Sweden with JA, he purchased 'Busy' and used that as a basis for a more scale-like car, resulting in the production of a delightful Alfa Romeo 158 in September 1950. Castings for this were priced at £1-5-0 as against the Tiger at 15/-, and the Alfa could be built with either a Twinshaft or single ended motor on a spur mount.

A new innovation was the 'Tiger Day' held at the club track in August 1950, with prizes for the fastest Oliver-powered car and the best Oliver/Howlett car. This gave due recognition to the scale aspect of the latter cars, and by using speed bonuses rewarded their builders' attention to scale and detail. A further addition to the range of scale bodies was a Ferrari, and it is believed that plans were in place for a BRM as well, although this does not appear to have made it into production. To give customers a range of options, all the cars could be supplied as raw or machined castings, or as completely finished and ready to run models.

1951 saw the introduction of the definitive MkII Tiger Twinshaft, abandoning the disc valve in favour of shaft induction, priced at £8-18-6. The earlier RV version would be retrospectively called the MkI. The new motor was used by Alex Snelling to set several new 2.5cc records, the highest speed being 84.11mph. As a measure of their success, Oliver engines finished in first, second and third places in the MG Trophy race as well as coming first and second in the MCA Nationals, and they also held all the 2.5cc National and Open records.

Tiger MkII

Lists and drawings from : J. A. OLIVER (Engineering), 136 Radford Rd., NOTTINGHAM, England

On test, the MkII motor produced 0.324bhp at around 15,000rpm, almost double the figures obtainable from the original side-port motor. Another complete car was added to the list in October, an Alfa available ready-to-run at £15-19-6 but only in the Twinshaft version, and two months later a near-scale Mercedes joined the growing list of models at the same price. During the same year the Olivers produced the first edition of a news-sheet called 'Tiger Tattle'. This was typed and duplicated and, as they were at pains to point out, only produced when time permitted and was definitely a 'gen' sheet, not a literary effort. The eight editions are full of technical and product information, tuning and set-up tips and good old-fashioned gossip, and cost just 1½d in postage. There was a hiatus between numbers seven and eight, covering the period that the company moved from Nottingham to Ferndown in Dorset, which was to become its home from 1954 to the present day.

Tiger Twin

At the Derby Open meeting and some other events in 1951, John S appeared with an experimental twin cylinder version of the Twinshaft, this time in a teardrop-style chassis. Essentially, this 5cc motor consisted of two complete Tigers back-to-back, with a common centre section that also served as the shaft valve for the right hand motor. The cranks of the two motors were set at 180 degrees apart so producing a most impressive noise and the car was no slouch either, reaching speeds of around 80mph. Later on, the motor was turned over so that the cylinders faced forward and it was installed in a semi-scale body.

Another entirely functional car, the Tiger Bomb, was planned for December '51 and was intended mainly for continental use with 3.25cc ('.19') motors. The top and bottom halves were symmetrical, and (as the name suggests) it did look rather like a bomb. This left little room internally, so it was originally planned to cast in the driving axle with pre-machined ends, although it was anticipated

"The Bomb"

that conventional Twinshafts might find more favour in the UK. In the end the castings were left plain, although there was always some uncertainty over which end was supposed to be the front!

The Olivers were always willing to embrace developments and ideas from customers, especially the Snelling brothers who were great experimenters and engine builders as well as the setters of numerous records with Oliver motors; indeed, the concept of the 'curly carb' venturi was credited to Alec Snelling. So successful were the 2.5cc MkIIs that Alec decided to liner one down to 1.5cc, immediately breaking the class record with it.

MkII 'Curly Carb'

After a conversation with Alec, JSO produced a prototype set of parts, which were introduced in May as the 1.5cc 'Cub' conversion kit for MkII motors at a price of 48/6. This kit consisted of a new liner, piston, gudgeon pin, contra-piston and venturi, with which it was claimed that racer Cyril Catchpole managed to complete a trackside conversion in around 8 minutes! Cyril also invented the 'Bottoms Up' concept, using two pans from the 'Two-Five' car, which was raced by his wife Joan to great effect including the setting of new class records. Oliver adopted the idea with a new casting for the top half, giving the resulting car the name 'Tiger Cub', although these models are still known to this day as 'Bottoms Up'. At this time new models were coming thick and fast, including another Harry Howlett-inspired design, an A6G Maserati.

Although by this time JSO had been at the forefront of 2.5cc racing for two years, this did not always sit well with the other competitors, as he was deemed by some to be a 'works' entrant and therefore against the amateur spirit of the sport; certainly, the MCA would not allow anyone from 'the trade' to take up an official position.

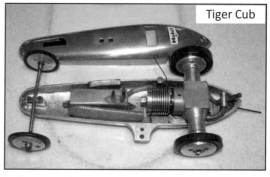
Tiger Cub

Despite this, he duly won the MG Trophy again, having not competed in 1949. By now, it seemed that 64mph was about the upper limit for JSO's own cars, but the Snelling brothers, with their highly developed and streamlined racers, were using Oliver motors to greater effect with Eric exceeding 70mph for both his runs at Cleethorpes, with JAO being very consistent too at 64mph for both of his. This would appear to signal the high point of the Oliver's personal racing careers as they now largely withdrew and were content to let their customers take on the mantle of success using their motors.

The change from the use of two-legged wire bridles to the almost universal 'pan handle' attachment forced the company to make new patterns for their cars; this seems to have started with the Tiger Cub in mid-1952. New versions of all the cars were available by 1953, and this is a useful means of establishing the possible date and history of any cars and castings that come onto the market today.

"Two Five"
Series 2

Outside the UK, the early 1950s saw Oliver motors dominating the 1.5 and 2.5cc Classes throughout Europe with the European, Swiss and Italian championships all won by Oliver-engined cars, with the Supertigre G20 being the only motor that challenged the Oliver in any way. The Twinshaft was also being constantly modified and tuned at this time by numerous competitors and installed in all manner of strange chassis configurations.

On September 28th 1958 Roland Salomon of Switzerland set a new World record at 150.25kph (93.3mph) with his 'Killer' car using an Oliver tuned by Phillip Rochat. Numerous other national and European Champions were also using Olivers, including Felice Riva and Stan Drayson who was campaigning a car that utilised the motor in a very different way; fellow-competitor Ian Moore had realised that there were two major limiting factors when using the Twinshaft layout; firstly, the difficulty in matching tyre sizes to engine revs with the direct drive, which Ian cured by returning to a geared drive, using bevel gears with the motor in a conventional pan.

A pair of
Shadows!

Secondly, to reduce the excessive frontal area, he machined the lugs off a single-ended motor to enable him to mount it in an extremely narrow bodyshell. On seeing this, JS reckoned that it was so thin it was almost a shadow, and so that became the car's name. It was eventually sold to Stan Drayson who campaigned it with great success.

Tiger II (Single-ended)

The move away from direct drive resulted in the majority of cars being fitted with single-ended motors on a spur mount in pans and chassis designed and built by the individual competitors themselves, such as Roland Salomon, Ken Procter, Les Williamson and Jack Cooke. A new version of the Tiger, the MkIII, had now been developed and was available for sale at £6-10-0, with the 1.5cc Tiger Cub version 10/- cheaper. The Twinshaft was still available too, but at a relatively pricey £9-18-6, albeit with wheels included.

Although highly effective, using an aero motor in a spur mount was not ideal and several different mounting systems were tried, many of which required the machining-off of the mounting lugs. One of the neatest and most well-engineered designs tried by the Olivers combined a Twinshaft-type centre casting with axle mounts cast in; to overcome the long shaft overhangs, the spur pinion was actually inside the front shaft housing. This must represent the pinnacle of integrated transmission design, although the concept does not seem to have made it into production.

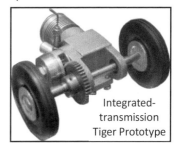
Integrated-transmission Tiger Prototype

Although the British interest in tethered car racing was diminishing, Oliver motors were still being run in competitions until eclipsed by the arrival of glow motors. The company continued to develop the Tiger motor by adding a 3.5cc version, as well as building numerous specials, one-offs and experimental engines. Oliver motors and their derivatives are still being run in vintage-style events, especially in Sweden, and their ongoing development has seen the records of the 1950s surpassed by a considerable margin.

JA at Orebo

John A Oliver died in 1988 but John S continued his involvement with the engines that bore his family name to the extent that in 2006, along with John Goodall, he travelled to Orebro in Sweden to compete again after more than 50 years out of the sport. Sadly, modern airlines and cars smelling of diesel fuel were not compatible so he was unable to take part, but the following year he was back, showing that he had lost none of his competitiveness and skill by putting in what was possibly his fastest run ever. In 2013, John Goodall, who also competes regularly with Oliver-based cars and engines achieved a long-held ambition and broke the 100mph barrier for the first time.

Inevitably, such a successful engine was going to be copied, either exactly, or by using similar design principles, and several British competitors built their own versions. In 1955-56 the Italian Oliver importers produced the ETI, a very near copy, some of which are still in use. In the old Eastern Bloc, the Twinshaft design was continued and refined with thousands of RYTM examples being used in car kits manufactured for schools and youth clubs. KMD also produced a Twinshaft but this was based on their aero-motor so had conventional mounting lugs, as did the very impressive Eureka; examples of all these motors are still regularly obtainable via eBay,

ED Hornet

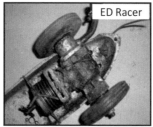

ED Racer

ED MkIII

dealers and swap-meets.

In the UK, good old British ingenuity was often invoked in order to avoid paying what was then a substantial sum for a genuine Oliver motor. This was achieved by pressing many other contemporary motors into service either by modifying them to a Twinshaft layout, or by running them with just one driven wheel and a slave axle. Proprietary parts would be grafted onto a homemade crankcase, or perhaps an entire motor cast or machined from the solid. These variations regularly appear for sale in genuine Oliver cars powered by ED, Elfin, ETA, AMCO and even venerable Mills motors rather than the 'real thing'.

In the 1990s there were several initiatives aimed at reviving the Oliver motors and cars. Ivan Prior started producing castings and complete cars by agreement with JS using the original patterns, and recently a Prior replica Mercedes sold for almost double the price of a complete and original Oliver version! John Oliver himself produced a limited run of Battleaxes and MkII motors, all of which were snapped up by collectors and competitors, and which now change hands for premium prices if they ever come up for sale. When Ivan withdrew from the market, Peter Hill took over the supply of castings under the Retro Racing Club banner, and continued to sell them for many years before Dave Coe took over the patterns and castings, with a view to setting up a business venture with his son. Ill-health precluded this, so the patterns were then passed to Eric Offen, who had a batch of each car made.

Oliver Car Patterns

Eric found this to be a more daunting venture than he was prepared for, so the patterns then went to Paul Ironmonger, who intended to produce castings and later, complete cars, and these may still be available today as a first batch of castings was in fact produced. Salvio Angelloni has also been producing castings for the Oliver range of cars but these are probably second or third generation and may not be from original patterns. All in all, considering the number of originals and replicas in existence, Olivers are probably the most numerous of any tethered car produced commercially.

On the engine front, the CS company in China went into production with both MkII Twinshaft replicas and single-ended motors, although the quality and performance of these were very variable; unfortunately, CS seems to have now given up most of its repro engine business. A few years ago Ian Russell ('Rustler') had a run of replica Jaguar motors made followed by the MkII Twinshaft; these are of excellent quality, and are eagerly sought-after if they now come onto the market.

In the case of CS and Rustler production the engines were informal copies of existing Oliver originals, but in 2008 Tom Ridley, then the owner of Clinthill Engineering, came to a formal arrangement with John Oliver to start producing genuine Oliver engines again using the original tooling. With Ridley's high quality engineering and input from JSO these motors are a worthy and highly-successful continuation of the Oliver name. In 2015 Tom sold his engineering business and was intending to continue production of Oliver engines as a stand-alone venture until this was precluded by his untimely death; however, it is believed that a member of his family has plans to reintroduce the 'Ridley Olivers'. Most recently, John Goodall has had a limited run of the MkII Twinshafts manufactured, also authorised by John Oliver.

On the commercial front we now see for sale original cars with original Oliver engines in place, original cars with alternative engine installations, reproduction castings with genuine motors and repro castings with repro motors. These possible variations present an absolute minefield for potential buyers but there are some helpful clues to distinguish non-original car castings from the originals, which tend to have a glittery silver finish rather than the matt grey of the reproductions. The originals are also noticeably larger and engine-wise, most of the original Oliver motors have a traceable serial number.

This brief history of the Oliver concern has been gleaned from contemporary reports, letters and magazine articles, but for a full, detailed, authoritative and extensively illustrated history of the Oliver family and their products we suggest you find a copy of 'The Olivers and a Tiger', a superb volume by John Goodall, a totally committed 'Oliver-phile'.

Sadly, John Oliver junior passed on in April 2016, and while we did discuss the concept of this article with him any errors within it must be our responsibility.

JAO at Old Warden

The authors are indebted to John Goodall for checking the text and for the generous loan of photos for us to copy and use, to Steve Betney for his valuable input and access to his collection and archive, and to Ron Reiter for photos of his Oliver cars.

'COMPLEX' - a <u>simple</u> twin-engined F/F model!
(by Eric Bulmer)

I decided to attempt this model as a change from the usual cabin-job. Why? Simply because it's there! There's nothing advanced in its design or construction, no pendulums, no mechanical engine inter-connection, in fact it doesn't live up to its name at all!

The important considerations were to find two engines of similar output and to make provision for single-engined flight while attempting to make both engines cut as near simultaneously as possible.

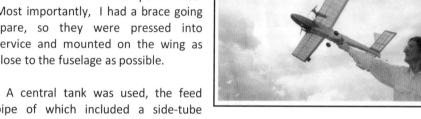

I chose a pair of Cox .049 Babe-Bee engines as, having reed-valves, they can be made to run in either direction, and are almost identical power-wise. Most importantly, I had a brace going spare, so they were pressed into service and mounted on the wing as close to the fuselage as possible.

A central tank was used, the feed pipe of which included a side-tube sealed with a removable clip: this pipe was then split to supply each engine. Removal of the clip allowed air into the system leaving the engines to run out the remaining fuel in their equal length lines. It looked untidy but worked a treat; as the French say of the derailleur cycle gears mechanism - "C'est brutale, mais ça marche" *("It's rough, but it works!")*

But, in spite of these precautions, what if one engine should quit before the other? To minimise the risk of a spin, both are offset 10° outwards and assisted by two large fins offset by the same amount, positioned in-line with the engines. This works well,

as one engine does usually cut out slightly before the other, and for extra stability I also added a small central fin and rudder too. The port engine is set up to run anti-clockwise and the starboard one clockwise using 6"x4" propellers 'turning inwards', for which the use of those Cox starter-springs is essential.

Once both engines are running they can be tuned by ear to approximately the same revolutions – for this, a passing jazz musician comes in handy – thank you Mikes (Parker and North) for your help here! To enable single-handed operation I added a wire loop at the sternpost through which a screwdriver anchors the model to the ground. Once both engines are running sweetly I remove the screwdriver from the clip and then launch.

First flight was at the BA Systems airfield at Brough, East Yorkshire and although one engine did cut appreciably before the other, 'Complex' flew on with no bother.

I entered it in the 2004 Bowden Contest and was the last to fly before the event was abandoned due to the increasingly heavy rain; the timekeeper actually asked me if I really wanted to fly – what a silly question!

Both engines started well within the two-minute allowance, and 'Complex' took off into the murk for a 9th place; alas, there was to be no second round. Photos of it being started and in flight appeared in 'Model Flyer' with a static picture appearing in the 'Aeromodeller' section of 'AMI'. If I ever feel the urge to build another, apart from adding radio-control, I would mount the engines on fuselage outriggers, as per the Dornier Do28.

...and here's a photo of that elegant little beast, taken at the Biggin Hill Air Fair in 1964 or 65 - its registration is D-IBAX, for you fellow plane-spotters (MM)!

But wait! What's this on page 202 of the May 1954 issue of 'Model Aircraft'? *(MM: Yes, that one on the table next to you with your coffee-cup resting on it!)* It's that Mr Hockey of Fordingbridge with a photo of his Junior 60, powered by two offset ED Bees both running anti-clockwise, fed from a central tank, and with just the one fin. It is, however, radio-controlled (ECC 95A Hard Valve, whatever that means!) but it maintains height on just one of those EDs...

And there's more: 'Photonews' in the July '53 issue of the same magazine shows Mr H.G.Sayers proudly putting his finger on the nose of a twin Mills 0.75 powered, 47" span free-flight flying-boat; it has no offset, a single fin and boasts "a stable flying performance (although rather fast)" – and the plot thickens further, egad   in the March '55 'Photonews' this flying-boat's span has magically increased to 72", and the two Mills, now *contra-rotating,* give the model "very slow but stable flight..." Are the models one and the same? We shall probably never know...

Nonetheless, as one multi-engined practitioner to another I take my woolly hat off to these two gentlemen for their endeavours, but - I simply must stop browsing through old magazines because, whatever I've seen or done, it's all seems to have been done before! The 'COMPLEX' specification is as follows: wingspan 49", chord 8", tailplane span 23", tailplane chord 5", fuselage length 40", weight 24.6 oz.

THE QI's HOT TIPS #1: Don't forget to scrub that tub!

When tissue is too heavy, why not cover your model with microfilm? Back in the '30s, modelling publications encouraged readers to make microfilm themselves in the family bath!

If you too want to go fully retro and make your own microfilm the authentic way, all you need is that tub and a bottle of Tricresyl Phosphate (TCP) to mix as a plasticizer with some spare nitrate dope. Finding the right mix is a matter of trial and error – the film's colour and weight will change across the spectrum from clear (too light) to red (too heavy) for model airframe use, so be prepared for some extended testing!

Once you've got your desired mixture, fill the bath then pour the mix onto the bathwater; it'll spread as wide and fast as a Trump Tweet. But how do you get the film out of the bath? Simples! Make a wire hoop from a clothes hanger, dip it into the bath and steadily withdraw it at an angle, just like a kiddie's bubble-blowing hoop, but bigger and a lot more dangerous!

Why dangerous? Oh, I think I forgot to mention that TCP (like dope) is toxic. TCP is used as a water-repellent and as an additive in engine turbine oil that, if it leaks into an airliner cabin pressurisation system, can cause 'Aerotoxic Syndrome', bringing on memory loss, depression and schizophrenia – not a good end to a holiday flight!

To use your sheet of microfilm, let it dry on the hanger, trim it with a soldering iron and then apply it gently to the airframe, using your very own spit as an adhesive. Yes, that's right, give the airframe a good licking! Naturally, after all that effort you'll need a nice hot bath to relax in, but do remember to scrub the tub out first. Oh dear, looks like Dad just beat you to the bath and is now slowly turning red all over and claiming to be Napoleon...

SUMMER FUN AT THE SEASIDE – FLYING WITH Dr MAGNUS
(by Kolley Kibber)

Think back to the year when you were nine or ten - for me that was 1960 - can you remember the annual family holiday at the seaside? I certainly can - the sun always seemed to be shining, ice-creams came in solid oblong blocks from Wall's, the wind-break flapped defiantly against Dad's best efforts to knock it into the shingle and everyone was on the lookout for the Daily Mail Mystery Man, hoping to win a fiver by challenging him with "You're Lobby Lud!"

Actually, all my ten-year-old self really needed for beach happiness (apart from bucket and spade and Tizer, of course) was my Skyroplane. The other lads could keep their kites and model boats; I just loved the sound of those celluloid wings rattling away as they spun in the breeze, lifting my plane higher and higher as I paid out on the line on that tiny fishing rod and reel,  zooming, diving and climbing until it was time to return to the boarding-house for tea and Mum's daily assault with wet hankies soaked in vinegar for my sunburn.

So who was Dr Magnus and how did he help my Skyroplane to get airborne on the beach at Littlehampton? Well, Heinrich Gustav Magnus (1802-1870) was an influential German scientist - readers may know that he was the first to explain the unexpected movement of balls that spin in flight through the air, an effect that also has a profound effect on planks and cylinders too, as we'll see shortly.

Back in 1960 I never gave any thought to why and how the Skyroplane's rotating wings worked because they just did, but in the course of compiling this Yearbook I discovered the fascinating aerodynamic theory behind it all, how easy it is to test out the theory for yourself, the possible benefits for the future of powered commercial flight, and the astonishing fact that the EU is pouring hundreds of thousands of Euros into research on this very topic.

Let's start by winding the clock back to 1942, when despite all odds the Aeromodeller magazine was still being published, even in the middle of World War Two. In the April issue a plan appeared for the 'Cyclogiro', a rather eccentric-looking machine based upon a full-sized proposal for a two-passenger aeroplane. The model is kept aloft and propelled by rotating wings à la Skyroplane via a convoluted rubber motor drive and gearbox.

Whilst enthusing about the possible benefits of rotating wing aircraft, the editor adds: "This little model aroused such a storm of controversy and interest in the editorial office that we felt quite justified in presenting it to readers even though it has never actually flown. It is not only interesting because it is a departure from the orthodox but also because there is more than a chance that some valuable data may be obtained from experimenting with a model of this type. In presenting this revolutionary design we offer a prize of £3-0-0 to the reader who obtains the most successful results based upon the principles in our drawing."

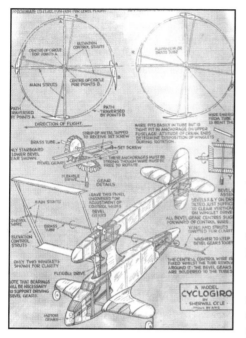

Now, £3.00 doesn't sound like a decent reward for resolving all those aerodynamic and constructional problems to produce a model without any balsa wood (it was all being used to build DH Mosquitoes at the time!), but it was actually a handsome sum worth very nearly £100.00 today. The Editor continued:

"In order to make a successful model it must be light and here we come up against a snag right away, for we need a most intricate system of gears to rotate the winglets. This is further complicated by virtue of the fact that they must revolve in the same direction. Flying trim is problematical but the centre of gravity should be under the axis of the winglets.

"Correct balance will have to be obtained by weights as you will not be able to shift the winglets fore and aft at will! It is suggested that an all-up weight of 2 ounces be aimed at and every effort made not to exceed this figure by too great a margin. Then, with the winglets revolving at about 900rpm, there is every chance that the model will leave the ground."

Given the minimal allowed weight and span parameters suggested, C of G uncertainty and complex gearing, that still looks like a hard way to earn three quid!

However, the Cyclogiro was certainly not the first example of an aeroplane with rotating wings, just as my toy Skyroplane in 1960 wasn't the last. Before WW1 the American inventor Butler Ames, foreseeing the need for spotter aircraft capable of operating from warships, designed and built the 'Aerocycle'. Looking like a pair of linen-covered cable-drums mounted on a kiddies' tricycle it got as far as sea trials on the back of the destroyer 'USS Bagley', but there's no record of it actually taking to the air, which was probably a matter of great relief to its test pilot...

However, the man who did most to get the rotating-wing concept into the air was Anton Flettner, a talented German engineer, inventor and pilot, although paradoxically he was more interested in its application to sea transport. When installed on a ship the rotating cylinders are mounted vertically and act as sails – quite successfully too, converting a side-wind into a stern-facing airflow. His invention is still being used today, albeit in small numbers. This specialised vessel delivers equipment and support to offshore wind-farms, so it's a very appropriate application! Flettner later designed helicopters for the Luftwaffe, but that's a story for Yearbook 17...

Stepping back onto dry land and getting back to model aviation, there was a period of renewed interest in Flettner's ideas in the 1950s and 60s, reflected in Frank Zaic's Year Books. The 1964-65 edition included an interesting collection of rotating-wing material from American and German sources as well as referring to an RAE Technical Note on the topic, so the principle was clearly being taken seriously within the scientific and modelling communities.

Looking at the aerodynamic theories behind the rotating wing, we still find a lot of reference to the art of baseball pitching and spin bowling, where (as per Magnus's original theory) putting a spin on a ball generates turbulence that interacts with the relative air pressure around it, and so imparts a curve to the ball's path in a semi-predictable way, with the proviso that humidity, barometric pressure and the texture of the ball's surface (as tampered-with by the bowler!) will also have an impact upon the ball's trajectory.

When the principle is applied to a cylinder, as long as the cylinder is turning faster than the relative airflow around it, then the net effect is lower air pressure on top and higher pressure underneath, generating a net upward force (lift).

If you exchange the cylinder for a flat plate it's possible to produce autorotation lift too - try the following experiment using something like a 12" sheet of 3" x 1/16th balsa to demonstrate the lifting capabilities of auto-rotation by first dropping it flat-

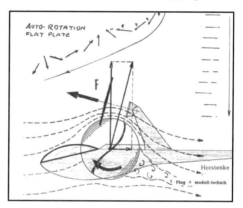

wise and counting the seconds it takes to reach the floor, then drop the same piece edgewise - although it may initially drop faster, it will soon start to rotate and move away from you and take almost twice as long to hit the carpet; the rotating sheet must therefore be producing lift somehow to delay the descent (see diagram), but if so how do you ensure that your rotating sheet wing never stalls when it reaches a position that's at 90 degrees to the airflow?

Well, the answer is to have a wing with at least two surfaces that are 'scooped' in some way like anemometer cups, and preferably formed into 'S'-shapes, as we see with our next model plan, Bruno Horstenke's 'Wirbelwind' from 1964.

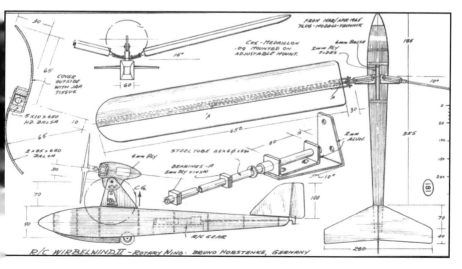

Heinrich's Whirlwind is effectively an autogiro version of my holiday Skyroplane, which is of course really a kite. However, they do share a common feature – their rotating wings are not directly powered, unlike the Cyclogiro in the Aeromodeller. This non-powered wing concept is brilliantly illustrated by Georges Chaulet in his charming illustrations around his 'Rotoplane' below.

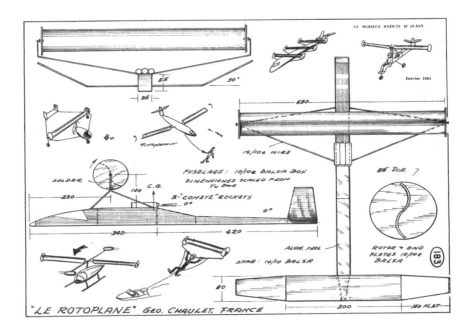

So that pretty much explains how and why a tethered or non-powered rotating sheet-wing works, but what about the ultimate application of Magnus's principle – the cylinder wing? Well, it's really just an extension of the applications we've looked at. To try it out for yourself, tape two light-weight plastic tumblers or KFC-type buckets together at their base, wrap an elastic band around them tightly where they are joined to act as a catapult, stretching it out from underneath, then let go – it will fly!

The final step is to power the rotating cylinders internally, and the next picture shows what you get – the Vectorkite!

Admittedly there's a small electric motor mounted on a gimbal underneath, but it's only used to control directional movement via radio control, not produce lift. Videos of this beast in flight can be found on YouTube.

So let's finish with a look at the future for rotating wing aircraft. In my introduction I mentioned that the EU had poured a significant amount of money into research on this topic which is called 'Cycloidal Rotor Optimized for Propulsion' (CROP). The project report says in summary:

"The CROP project introduces an innovative propulsion system for aircraft based on the cycloidal rotor concept, using an integrated approach that includes the electric drive train, airframe integration and an environmentally friendly energy source.

"The cyclorotor concept offers several potential advantages in comparison to traditional vertical takeoff and landing or fixed wing air vehicles. The rotating wing creates lift and thrust when the blades move backward with respect to the vehicle's direction of flight. Furthermore, the rotation speed and pitching of the cyclorotor do not need to increase with vehicle speed.

"A multidisciplinary research team from five European countries worked to demonstrate a propulsion system that would enable air vehicles to take off like a helicopter and fly at high speeds like aircraft. The CROP project was funded with more than half a million Euros by the European Commission.

"Specifically, CROP project partners showed the combined effect of a leading edge vortex and what is called a plasma-enhanced cycloidal thruster using computational fluid dynamics models and numerical analysis. To achieve a lower weight-to-power ratio, the integration of a low-weight electric drive train into the system was explored.

"By the end of the project, CROP

"By the end of the project, CROP optimised a four-rotor lab model and demonstrated proof-of-concept for an electrically powered cyclogyro. This breakthrough concept is leading the way to innovative air vehicle designs with improved performance and reduced environmental impact."

So I wonder how long it will be before we see young lads on the beach at Littlehampton flying a model with a plasma-enhanced cycloidal thruster as a power-source? Not next year, I'd guess, but never mind, whilst we're waiting it's good to know that the Skyroplane has a direct descendant that our kids can have fun with until those next generation supertoys come onto the market – enter the Aerokite!

The makers say: *"Aerokite is a wind toy that looks like a plane and flies like a kite. Aerokite has rotating wings that create a motor-like sound and provide excellent lift in all wind conditions. The wing span is 27" and comes ready to fly with little adjustment necessary. Aerokite is easy to fly, just unroll some line, hold the Aerokite high against the wind until both wings rotate rapidly and let it go. The Aerokite is suitable for kids ages 5 and up and can be flown in any open space (backyards, beaches, parks, etc)"*

Perfect – I'm sure that Dr Magnus would approve! I've still got my bucket and spade, so let's pick up an Aerokite and some Tizer at the newsagent (yes, Tizer is still made) and practice our rotary-wing aviation, ready to celebrate the good Doctor's 150th anniversary in 2020. Who knows, we might even catch my old mate Lobby Lud and win a fiver!

Acknowledgement is made to the owners of the various trademarks and products we've recalled from my youth and mentioned in this article, as well as our thanks to the original publishers of the various plans and photographs I've used for illustrative purposes to explore the Magnus effect.

The Keil Kraft Pirate
(by Andrew Longhurst)

It's 1960, and the scene is Cranford Park, West London. There's me, aged 12, and my Dad with our new Keil Kraft Pirate. The Mills .75cc diesel starts, the boy launches, the plane rolls in to the right and crashes. Try again, the Mills buzzes, they launch, same result. Try again, a stall this time and another crash. Eventually they give up and go home. That KK Pirate will never fly again.

Sigmund Freud was a wily old fox. He understood the extraordinary effect such childhood failures can have. The subconscious stores it up, filed carefully under "Not to be forgotten". When the conscious mind goes blank, the subconscious seizes the chance to fill the void. Its files are sometimes ignored for a long time until circumstances are right. Chasing girls and bringing up families inevitably suppresses memories of childhood failure, but if as a youngster you failed to succeed at something that was important to you, that file will be extracted, dusted off and sent upstairs time and time again. Eventually, suppressing it becomes more difficult than trying again and succeeding, or if not succeeding, then just understanding.

So it was that in the early 90's I was editing SAM Yearbook No7 and commissioning articles. There it flashed again, that annoying image of the blue fuselage with white wings rolling over into the grass and the sudden silence. As a boy I thought I had built it really well so why wouldn't it fly? I spoke to the late John Godden to get him to explain how this could possibly have happened. He told me in his broad Yorkshire accent, "That Mills were right too powerful for a model only 33 inches span. Likely that was t'problem." He duly contributed an article advising Mills owners to build something larger, so it wasn't my fault after all! If only I'd known that

earlier I could have forgotten the whole debacle and got on with my life...

But it proved a diagnosis without a cure. Still it niggled. When I returned to free flight in the early eighties, I was totally obsessed with rubber models but somehow in that time, I acquired not one, but two copies of the Pirate plan. I would often get one out and look at it in disbelief. Why? Well you see, the Pirate was designed by Bill Dean, the man guilty of introducing me to the narcotic of aeromodelling.

His exquisitely illustrated Eagle Book of Balsa Models (later the Solarbo Book) hooked me for life. How could it be that this master of the art, whose beautiful designs always flew, drew up something that failed to get airborne? And then there was the Keil Kraft slogan, "KK Models are designed to fly!" But there on the plans are details of how to fit three different engines, all of which I am now told are unsuitable. There's the Mills .75, then there's the similar Amco .87, and lastly the rather different 1cc ED Bee.

At the time of writing this piece I'd weaned myself off my addiction to rubber power and had already won a couple of Mini Vintage events with small diesels, so I was looking at the Pirate with a bit more knowledge. Like for instance, I'd learned that the tiniest misalignment of the fin would be punished mightily! Was that the problem? These days there would be no argument that the Pirate is only suitable for .5cc engines such as the DC Dart or ED Baby.

However, those engines weren't available until the fifties and the Pirate was designed in late '48 or early '49, so the kit advertising just said that it was for engines up to 1cc. Was this reckless mis-selling, which nowadays would earn a slap from the Trading Standards, or would it really fly with the suggested hardware up front?

Eddie Keil was the owner of the biggest kit company in Europe and was well known for his insistence on witnessing test flights. I can just imagine the scene as Bill Dean demonstrated his new design...

Eddie: This one looks very nice. I see you've used that wretched Amco again.

Bill: Yes sir, but it's a little sweetie...

Eddie: I don't like the Amco, not many of our customers have them. A Mills is better, everyone's got a Mills!

Bill: Well, Amco gave this one to me and besides, it's got a built in fuel cut off which saves time when I am doing all these prototypes for you. But don't you worry, sir; I'm going to show the Mills on the plan as well!

(The engine burps into life. Bill fiddles with the engine controls then launches it into a blue sky all set about with puffy white clouds. The model climbs away and circles twice. The engine dies and it glides down to a three-point landing on the perfectly-mown grass of Eaton Bray)

Eddie: That was beautiful – well done! We'll get that kitted as soon as possible. When can you get the plan to me?

Bill: Will next week do?

Eddie: That's fine – I was thinking we could call it the Pirate...

Bill: Oh that's brilliant sir, the youngsters will love it! Only you could have come up with a name like that.

Eddie: Yes quite. (pause...) I was having luncheon with Henry J Nicholls the other day and he said that he was selling a lot of these little ED Bee diesels that have just come out. If we could show how to fit the ED as well as the others we would have a really big market for this one. Yes, we could sell a lot of these Pirates. Can you show the ED Bee on the plan as well?

Bill: Er, yes sir, but there are some problems with the ED, it's rather heavy and the air intake is...

Eddie: (not listening) Terrific, just make the necessary tweaks and we will get it out as soon as possible.

Bill (resignedly): OK sir... (thinks - he'll want me to put a Dooling 29 in it next!)

I'm sure this story is apocryphal because more than anything, Eddie wanted his kit models to fly, hence his slogan "Designed to Fly", but enthusiasm sometimes knows no bounds!

How do I know Bill used the Amco in the prototype? Well, he used it in his earlier Slicker and Southerner Mite designs and I suspect he transferred it straight into the next power model he was working on, which was the Pirate. This table below shows how the three engine installations shown on the plan compare. Significantly, the Amco is the least powerful option although engine tests in those days were probably not very accurate. In particular, the Mills tested must have been supercharged or something.

I don't have an Amco but I do have a Mills and an ED Bee. If I'm going to build this thing I might as well choose the biggest challenge and go for the Bee because the rear disc induction ED is not only relatively heavy, it's also more powerful than the other two motors, which are side-ports.

Engine	CC	Oz	Bhp
Mills .75	0.75	1.75	0.060
Amco .87	0.87	2.00	0.045
ED Bee 1.0	1.00	3.00	0.065

A quick check showed that the Bee was revving a 7x4 at 9700 against 7800 for my rather feeble Mills. The extent of the challenge can be illustrated three ways:

- The 'Iota', a successful 1950 competition power model designed specifically for the Bee, is of 200sq.ins wing area as opposed to 135sq.ins for the Pirate

- Calculations based on my 1970s career in control line, where speeds are always known, show that the ED would be able to tow the Pirate straight and level at around 40mph. That's about three times the glide speed

- The Bee can produce a static thrust of about 6oz (168g) and more than that in the air. The weight of the Pirate is only 7oz (190g) ready to fly. "OMG!" as our kids would text today!

As designed, the installation of any of these engines in the Pirate is gloriously impractical because they all have rear air intakes penetrating the first bulkhead which makes choking impossible and cleaning out oil residue very difficult. Additionally, the use of high curved sides to the engine bay means that bolting the engine in is a problem unless it is already in place when you build the cowling.

I remember as a boy looking at the two thick blocks of balsa for the cowling cheeks and wondering how it all went together. In the end I just made a cut out for the lugs and glued them in on top of the engine. Next I got out the sand paper and filled the engine with balsa dust. Everyone knows that Mills love firing up on balsa dust. Some say it's as good as lycopodium powder! *(MM: what's that then? Well today, the its principal use is to create flashes or flames that are large and impressive but relatively easy to manage safely, in magic and theatrical SFX. Well, I never knew that!)*

The rest of the plane is simple and beautiful. The one complexity is how Bill tried to deal with the CG problem. In order to have a stylish fuselage reminiscent of a full size light plane and also accommodate the engine air intake, the wing had to overhang the engine. Bill decided to solve this by cutting out a section of the leading edge. It's no problem for me to deal with now but as a boy it was difficult, especially with the sheet covering on top.

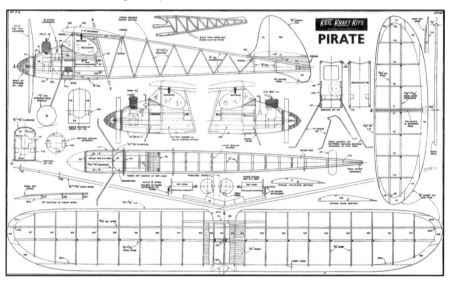

Now, all the stuff I've written above is in the past, and at this very moment I'm standing on the blasted heath of Chobham Common, well known to gobble up small toy planes in its maw of heather, gorse and swamp. Hand glides show it to be woefully under-elevated on the 30% CG shown on the plan.so I invest 2 pence in the tail to get it back to 55%. It glides, hmmm, sort of.

I start the Bee equipped with a massive 9x6 installed back to front. It climbs straight at 30 degrees and then glides tight left. I glue a bit of 1/16 square on the right side of

75

the fin to steady the glide and perhaps get a power turn. Start the Bee, off it goes, climbing the same but the glide is not so spirally.

This is going much better than I'd dared hope, especially after my friend had regaled me with tales of how his Bee-powered version swooped about all over the sky. I reverse the prop knowing this will increase the thrust quite a lot. Off it goes again, this time climbing steep right, fast and steady. I can't believe this. I fly it again and it's just fine, although the glide is steep.

The plan says use a 7x5 prop. Today, we would think of this as ideal for the Bee but in those days a larger prop might be used; for instance, the 'Iota' used an 8x4½. The Pirate has been so steady, so keen to fly, that what the heck? Let's go for it!

I bolt on the 7x5 and launch it at 45 degrees. It goes straight up and then starts a loop but no, it half rolls, turns 180 degrees very tight in a vertical bank, then it goes straight up again. The twirl is repeated twice more before the engine cuts and it glides down rather nicely, relieved to get rid of that oversized 9x6.

DEAR BILL DEAN – WHY EVER DID I DOUBT YOU?
FORGIVE ME, PLEASE!

Jetex Hawker Hunters at 60mph and 100psi!

(by Arthur Burch, as told to Roger Simmonds and Brian Jones)

"In early 1953 my friend Dan Barker and I were stationed at 32 MU RAF St. Athan. We were given the task of producing a model flying display to be used on RAF recruiting stands at big exhibitions and shows around the country. The first of these was to be the Earls Court Radio Show in late 1953. This was to be followed by a stand at the Schoolboys' Own Exhibition in early 1954 and many other shows in 1954 and 1955. An article appeared in the Model Aircraft Magazine in February 1954 that described our stand at the Schoolboys Own Exhibition.

"Our Station Commander at the time was Group Captain A.R. Saw; he gave us the full backing of all the facilities on 32 MU, including our own workshop, and we were taken off all normal duties to work full time on the project. The station departments involved in the making of this display included the machine shop, the chrome-plating section, the carpenters shop, the instrument, electrical and radio sections, as well as the Motor Transport section that provided two 'Queen Mary' transporters to convey all our equipment.

"Our first attempt at a Round-the-Pole (RTP) model was an electric ducted fan-powered Boulton Paul BP 111, an experimental delta. Although it did fly, our fan was very inefficient and despite putting 48 volts through the 24 volt motor, there wasn't much power. One of us then came up with the idea of using a compressed air-jet, with the air supply being fed to the plane down a plastic tube from a rotating banjo union on the centre pole. This proved to be the answer and performance was good, providing we had an ample supply of air!

"About this time, the Hawker Hunter was about to enter service and there was a 'Jetex' Kit for this aircraft on the market. it had a span of around 18 ins. and a length of 20 ins, which seemed to be an ideal choice provided we could adapt it to our needs. To help make the models more representative of the Hunters coming into service we were given the serial numbers of the first batch of aircraft - WT 555 to WT 560.

"These models were intended for solid fuel 'Jetex' rocket motors using an aluminium 'augmenter tube' running the length of the fuselage. With the Jetex motor blasting down the tube, air was drawn into the tube by the jet's exhaust which increased the thrust available over that which the motor alone could produce. We made use of this feature in conjunction with our air-jet, as you can see from the drawing. In order to supply sufficient air for two aircraft to perform together, we had to use three substantial electric compressors, of the size a garage/workshop would need, producing 100psi.

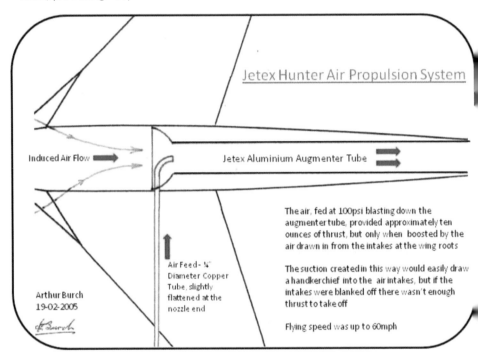

Jetex Hunter Air Propulsion System

Induced Air Flow

Jetex Aluminium Augmenter Tube

The air, fed at 100psi blasting down the augmenter tube, provided approximately ten ounces of thrust, but only when boosted by the air drawn in from the intakes at the wing roots

Air Feed- ¼" Diameter Copper Tube, slightly flattened at the nozzle end

The suction created in this way would easily draw a handkerchief into the air intakes, but if the intakes were blanked off there wasn't enough thrust to take off

Arthur Burch
19-02-2005

Flying speed was up to 60mph

"To make our Hunters more realistic I designed a retracting undercarriage, powered by a 24 volt electric motor. This worked on the screw-jack principle, where the nut cannot be pushed along the thread. This gave effective locking in both up and down positions as per my drawing, which shows how it operates. The double worm drive reduction gearbox was designed and built by a skilled instrument maker, Vic Quelch, who also made all the brass end fittings for the push rods.

"The centre pole had as its base a supercharger impeller from a Rolls-Royce Merlin with the blades machined off. We used to fly two aircraft in formation and each plane had its own swivelling head on the pole. This banjo type connection fed the air to the model via a ¼" neoprene tube, while three slip rings fed the electric supply down fine wires to the undercarriage motor.

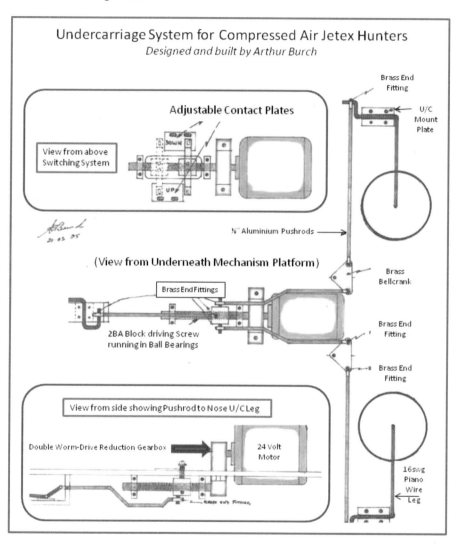

Undercarriage System for Compressed Air Jetex Hunters
Designed and built by Arthur Burch

Brass End Fitting

Adjustable Contact Plates

U/C Mount Plate

View from above Switching System

¼" Aluminium Pushrods

(View from Underneath Mechanism Platform)

Brass Bellcrank

Brass End Fittings

Brass End Fitting

2BA Block driving Screw running in Ball Bearings

Brass End Fitting

View from side showing Pushrod to Nose U/C Leg

Double Worm-Drive Reduction Gearbox

24 Volt Motor

16swg Piano Wire Leg

"The 'airfield' was 30ft in diameter with a flat outer runway, built in 8 sections for ease of transport. Incorporated into the outer runway were retractable guide rails that were used to steer the nose wheel of the model from the runway to follow a fixed rail on the taxi-way up and over to the centre part of the airfield, where there were two solenoid-operated chocks. You can see both the rails and the chocks on the photo showing WT557 up against them. In the centre of the airfield was a chequered runway control van with red & green lights, and a hangar with a spare aircraft parked within it.

"The control panel was about eight feet long with three operator positions for two pilots and a ground marshall, who controlled the retractable guide rails, the runway controller's lights (red & green), the chocks and the sound system. Each pilot had two control levers, the throttle and the undercarriage selector, and he also had a voltage control, a warning light and an air pressure gauge.

1: The airfield, hangar and operator stations

"The outer model would fly at up to 60 mph - it was very tricky to fly two in formation due to the different radii of the flight paths - they flew at quite different speeds. With around 10ozs thrust they accelerated quickly to flying speed and landing took some care to avoid heavy arrivals. The show attracted a great deal of interest and hopefully fulfilled its purpose by helping the recruiting policy of the RAF; in its 'Heard at the Hanger Doors' editorial feature, the Aeromodeller magazine of March 1954 was enthusiastic about the ingenuity deployed in both the construction and operation of the display, to the extent that it actively encouraged its younger readers to consider a career in the RAF!

Including research time, building and testing, the project took the best part of a year to bring to fruition.

The photos accompanying this article give some idea of the scale of the display, both static and flying. In the picture below, Arthur Burch can be seen standing and

giving instruction to a seated man wearing glasses, who is none other than the soon-to-be knighted Frank Whittle, leader of the British jet engine design and development initiatives at the time.

Arthur's involvement in the project sadly came to an end when he was hospitalised for 15 months. He put the time to good use

2: Sir Frank Whittle spools up a Hunter...

by building more than 40 models whilst incarcerated, but by the time he was sufficiently well to resume his duties the RAF had decided that the recruiting initiative had run its course, and had discontinued it.

ANDERS DEURELL'S WAKEFIELDS
(by Andrew Longhurst)

Anders Deurell was a Swedish Wakefield flyer competing throughout the golden period of the eight-ounce formula. He was overshadowed by the great Swedish Wake flyers of the period, particularly the double World Champion Arne Ellila. Unlike his Swedish contemporaries he rejected a light boxy fuselage in favour of something more complex, creating wonderfully original models which flew well enough, but were perhaps hampered by their weight. We have three of his unique designs to remember him by, the Taifun, the Monsun and his un-named 1950 Wakefield...

My thanks go to Sten Persson for providing two articles, Mrs Google for translating them and Devon Sutcliffe for his critique on the Monsun. The articles have had to be edited to fit in the yearbook, but full text is available from the author of this article.

The 1939 Taifun Wakefield

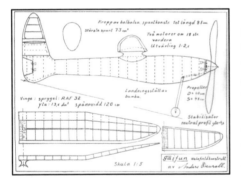

Anders built this original model in the spring of 1939, a streamlined Wakefield with full-body planking and a gearbox in the nose. The model was quite well documented in the magazine 'Flying'. The photo on page 84 features Anders launching at the Vingernes Winter Contest in March 1939, making the best flight of the day with an impressive 5:10.

Hans Karlsson wrote in 2015/16 of his attempt to re-create the Taifun – he says: "The drawing is short of a plan view of the fuselage so this had to be calculated. The largest dimension would have been 120 mm high and 80 mm wide to meet the cross-section rule. The spinner gives us the width at the nose while at the back the height of the two rubber hooks seems to have been 50 mm, so I decided that the width at

this point must be 25 mm. The cross-section changes only slightly between the adjacent formers so I made a set of templates that were adjusted until I was satisfied, starting with simple cardboard templates attached to a piece of corrugated board. My mould was constructed just like this, and probably it

was much the same as Deurell would have used. The fuselage is built in two halves, with the original planked with 1mm balsa, although I used 1.5m for the replica, cut into strips to fit the shape. Stark and Sundström wrote that building a shell body requires a jig and add that only the most skilled will succeed in building such a structure. Well, I now belong to that most skilled shell-body-building club!

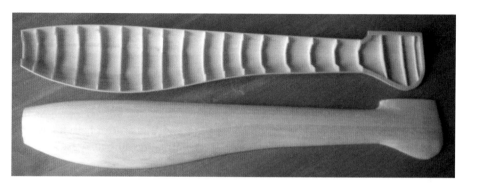

The difficult moments are to fit in the last plank, especially at the tail which incorporates the lower part of the fin and the double-curved part between the front of the fin and the upper surface of the body. The first half of the fuselage weighed 28.4 grams. The other half is easier as you already have the experience you would like to have had when you made the first half; once the two body halves are finished you have every right to feel really, really satisfied. Put the halves together and see how well they fit each other. Sit down, sip something good and enjoy the moment!

Even before joining the halves, you can get a sense of how rigid this construction is. But, before gluing them we must build in mounting brackets for the retracting landing gear. The operating mechanism with its spring is internally mounted and then the two shells are glued together around it, so it's not ideal if anything goes wrong. Two plugs of plywood and suitable reinforcements are also required for the rear motor hooks and these are inserted through a cut-out at the back with appropriate internal reinforcements.

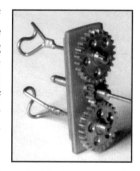

The front mounted gears in the original model are made of steel with the gear teeth 18 and 45. These gears must be ordered, so available brass 16 and 31 gears were used instead. I obtained Firma Kuggteknik gears which are really nice but are very thick with really large hollow hubs, so I split a wheel into two in the lathe using a thin saw blade!

The wing has a RAF 32 profile with a flat middle section, and two strong tapered wing tips. The LE has a torsion nose of 1 mm balsa. The wing pylon is streamlined hollow balsa that is attached to the underside of the wing and slides along on the body where it is guided by a triangular shaped piece of hardwood which simultaneously provides attachment for the rubber bands attaching the pylon to it. The wing is then attached to the pylon with more rubber bands as usual.

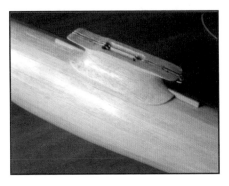

The stabilizer and the upper part of the fins are removable and were attached on the original by bands. I used a press stud and a locating pin which fits into one of the holes drilled in a thin aluminium block! This complex arrangement allows for adjustment of the angle of attack of the stabilizer and also a fuse operated pop up trailing edge DT.

Trimming and flight

The finished model weighed 250 grams without rubber as follows:
Body with landing gear legs and legs: 123g
Wing: 43g
Pylon: 12g
Stabilizer: 13g
Noseblock (gear, propellers and spinner): 57.5g

Definitely overweight for a Wakefield, but so was the original. In this case, the two motors are geared in such a ratio that each rubber motor should be of normal cross section. I used 20 or 24 strands of 3mm. Downthrust was as shown on the plan plus a little right thrust as well. After initial test glides the wing position was consistent with both drawing and photos of the original model. Some negative incidence was found to be needed on the tailplane.

The initial flight attempts were made with two 'half' engines, i.e. half the hook distance and the rest a rod. The Taifun rose in a nice right circle looking promising despite its being well overweight. If I did it again, I would save weight but on the whole, I am very pleased with it!

The Monsun Wakefield of 1946/49

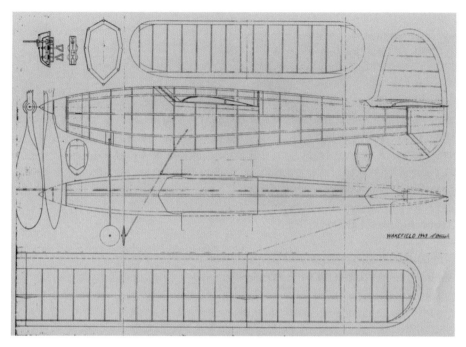

WAKEFIELD 1949 *MONSUN*

Now over to Devon Sutcliffe to describe the Monsun Wake: The September 1949 issue of *Aeromodeller,* in their report on the Wakefield Finals, contains two interesting photographs. The first shows 'a beautiful straight take off by Deurell', while the second shows the same model in closer detail, as it was being prepared for flight. Unfortunately for Deurell, the Wakefield takeoff was not converted into a substantial flight, and his times were only 7.4 and 20 seconds, for an aggregate of 27.4 seconds and 76th place. No third flight time was recorded.

His model departed from the traditional Scandinavian boxy rectangular fuselage and instead utilised a basic tissue covered octagonal section with 1.5mm sheet formers and eight stringers of 3mm X 3mm (the plan shows a later fully streamlined version covered later). Overall length of the fuselage was 780mm, and it was probably assembled on an internal jig. The shoulder wing was mounted just above the thrust line, and extended right through the fuselage with a removeable fairing. In profile, the fuselage was quite deep at the rear, as the two rubber motors were mounted vertically and were spaced well apart. A twin undercarriage of 1.5mm wire plugged into tubes located in the fuselage was complemented by 37.5mm wheels. The single fin was relatively large, but of low aspect ratio. It was of symmetrical section and merged into an underfin which formed part of the rear fuselage structure.

The wing was a one-piece structure with a span of 1080mm, and a chord of 135mm. It featured a flat centre section, and employed a constant chord, apart from the tip being almost semi-circular in shape. Tip dihedral was 100mm. Although the wing section was not named, it obviously was one of the SI ranges being thin and featuring slight undercamber, with 1mm leading edge sheeting extended rearward on the top surface for 30mm. There was one internal spar of 4mm X 3mm, situated at 60% of the chord. Ribs appear to be of 1.5mm sheet, and were pitched at 30mm.

The tailplane was of sparless construction, with a similar planform to the wing. Span was 440mm and the chord 105mm. The section was not named, but it was thin and undercambered, and probably also from the SI series. Ribs were also pitched at 30mm. A tipping tail DT was fitted.

The double blade freewheeling propeller of 440mm diameter was` carved from a 55mm X 35mm block. Twin motors were employed, operating through gears in the noseblock. However, they were not return gears, as they fed into a smaller gear mounted on the propeller shaft. No motor size was quoted on the plan, but hints can be derived from an earlier Deurell design.

The 1949 model was similar layout to the 1946 model, save that the wing was located on top of the fuselage rather than in a shoulder position. 'Monsun' featured a 430mm diameter propeller, and this was driven by gears stepped down 1:2.5, and powered by two motors of 16 strands, presumably 6mm in width. Performance was quoted to be in the 3-4 minute range.

Deurell's 1950 'Un-named' Wakefield

In 1950 Deurell made a quantum change with his new design. This continued the use of a streamlined fuselage, but he combined this with a retractable undercarriage and a folding propeller, and changed from a geared motor to a straight motor. With the elimination of the gears, the fuselage was lengthened by 75mm to 850mm, and the structure changed to a fully sheeted oval section. The shape was also changed,

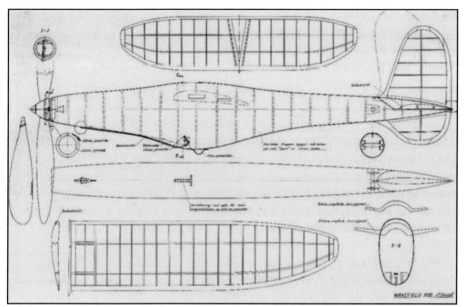

with a distinct bulge being created on the lower profile. This was the location point for the single 1.25mm wire leg undercarriage, which retracted forwards. A twin-bladed folding propeller was built into a spinner with a diameter of 440mm. Deurell wrote a rather quirky article for the 'Hobby-People' magazine in February 1951 entitled, "This is not how to do it!" which suggests that he was not completely satisfied with his new model. He wrote:

"Are you going to build in solid balsa?" If your answer is "Yes!" then I recommend that you hang your model on the wall as soon as it's finished, because once it has crashed you will, like me, no longer be able to enjoy looking at its beautiful shape - I do have to say that I've never managed to build another creature like this one!

"If we start from the nose, it had (while it still existed!) a folding propeller set up to stop so that the blades would fold as closely as possible alongside the body and so reduce turbulence. We then might have a look below the fuselage, where two small wheels are tenderly pressed together and half lost within it. Each wheel is mounted on a piano wire leg. If you pull them down they obediently follow, but still they hang together – they don't part until they have come out so far that their legs are perpendicular to the fuselage. When you put down the model you must keep its legs apart until it stands firmly on the ground. When we lift up the model the legs close again and retract forward halfway into the fuselage. If we now go back along the fuselage we get to the belly, made both in accordance with Rule $L^2/100$ and my endeavours to keep the weight down as much as possible. Moving along the model's back we come to the wings, which have dowels that cross the fuselage. An internal rubber band between the wing halves holds them tight against it, with no external rubber bands needed.

We can see that the 10% thick wing section is rather cambered, though actually not enough - I will come to why that is in a moment - and the wing is finished with a rounded ellipsoid tip. If we go back further, we will come to the stabilizer and the fin, which are built into a cut-out in the body's upper side. The front of the stabilizer is attached to the body in such a way that it can tip up 45 degrees when the dethermalizer fuse burns through.

The fuselage section is oval, being 45 mm in diameter at both the front former and the rear motor anchorage. The fuselage is built in two halves on a wooden board, using 1x3 mm balsa formers with their broad sides facing outwards, making them less vulnerable in case of motor breakage, and placed at 3 cm intervals. The fuselage planking is made from 1 mm balsa, reduced to 0.75 mm after sanding, and finished with three coats of dope. Weight, including ply and balsa reinforcements, is 44 grams, while the total weight of the model is 240 grams, including 120 grams of pre-tensioned rubber, driving the propeller directly without gears.

I'll finish with a few words about its one and only flight. Its consistently streamlined shape combined with the chosen aerofoil made it sweep along like a fighter plane, displaying a very low sinking speed. If I had used thicker and more curved profiles I could have reduced the speed, but otherwise it had a very good ability to turn in any direction with the same rudder setting, between right and left turns. However, it did not live to get old - at first, I had the impression that it was very stable, but I was wrong; it's now well messed-up, and a total write off!"

Wakefield 'Twin Gull'

RPH - The Wisp, the Wideye and the Duke of Edinburgh!
(by Mike May)

Ladies and gentlemen, before you go into meltdown, let me reassure you that I'm not going to write about those remotely-piloted plastic four-rotor drones that you can buy today on the internet for £20, although they do get a mention in passing right at the end! No, this is about a 1970s initiative by Westland Helicopters, using inspirational adaptations of vintage model aircraft technology to help in the defence of the realm; it's about their Remotely Piloted Helicopter (RPH) programme. I wrote the first version of this article a few years ago whilst editing a newsletter for the Customer Support division of AgustaWestland (now Leonardo Helicopters) for whom I worked for over 40 years.

In compiling it I had access to the company archives and was also able to meet many of the people who were involved in this secret initiative back when loon pants and sideburns ruled the day. I'm pleased to say that I've had the blessing of the company's PR department to reuse this material for the SAM35 Yearbook.

The Mission

At the time of the Cold War (1947-1991), the biggest perceived threat to the West was a massed Russian tank invasion of Europe. NATO would have needed accurate artillery and rocket fire to repel the Red Army, for which 'spotters' would have been essential, to call the range and direction of targets and the 'fall of shot' (accuracy of aim) of the NATO gunners. This isn't a new thing; back in WW1 on the Western Front, this task was carried out by observers in tethered balloons behind the front lines, but that was a very exposed and dangerous method and quite unsuitable for use in the jet-age - something radically new was needed.

The Westland Solution – Birth of the 'Mote'

To address this need, Westland began to develop RPH concepts for battlefield surveillance; helicopters are highly mobile, can loiter at low level, hide behind trees and buildings and operate from any patch of open ground. To gain experience, the company funded the construction of a prototype called the '**Mote**', which was built initially from aeromodelling components bought from the model shop then in Yeovil's Princes Street – (does anyone remember the Digi-

Hangar?) The lucky proprietor sold a lot of twin glow-plug engines and state-of-the-art R/C equipment thanks to this project! The Mote first flew on 13 June, 1975, after which the design was steadily developed to improve its integrity and reliability by substituting Westland-designed components for many of the original aeromodelling parts.

The Mote went on to become a flying test bed for an electronic gyro-based control system for use on the '**Wisp**', the next generation of Westland RPH. The Mote made a total of 37 flights before it was retired, and it's now on display in the Helicopter Museum at Weston-super-Mare, as are most of the other Westland RPHs described in this article. It's well worth a visit!

The 'Wisp' hovers in...

The Mote configuration of twin engines driving co-axial rotors was continued in the '**Wisp**'. This was a short-range surveillance RPH, weighing 70 lb, powered by two 5hp petrol engines, and was able to carry a television camera. The 'fuselage' was a squashed doughnut (OK, toroidal!) shape with the rotors protruding from the top and four fixed landing legs splayed out underneath.

The electronic gyro-based flight control system developed and flight-tested on the Mote was used in the Wisp to establish its performance characteristics, with the first flight being made in December 1976. The second and third aircraft flew in 1977 and carried small television cameras, movable in elevation and stabilized in pitch and roll.

Two of these RPHs were used to support follow-on development programmes, one going to the RAE Farnborough for flight trials, and one famously meeting a bemused Duke of Edinburgh with young Princes Andrew and Edward at the 1978 Farnborough Air Show. This is the photo that made the front page of many national newspapers!

The Wisp could easily be handled by two persons and was intended to operate from anywhere that a Land Rover could reach. It was designed and hand-built in

Yeovil together with its advanced automatic stabilization system but it had its limitations, so the next generation was already in development – the **'Wideye'**.

Wideye & Sharpeye – now it's getting serious!

With all these developments, it's easy to forget that there was no GPS system at the time to track the position of the RPH, and no secure satellite communications to relay command signals. Westland was therefore also developing sophisticated narrow-band radio control systems, RPH autonomous flight rules, and most importantly inertial navigation equipment to turn the RPH airframe into a mission-capable weapons system. Here's a

picture of the sophisticated (for the era) camera on the follow-on Wideye RPH, and a photo of the interior of its mobile control vehicle.

Encouraged by the successful start to its RPH programme provided by the Mote and Wisp, Westland then decided to develop a complete medium-range unmanned aerial surveillance system.

The next airframe, called Wideye ("**Wide-Eye**") grew taller, looking rather like a large Easter egg topped off with contra-rotating rotors. Westland chose this design because its pilot would not have to worry about steering it laterally, but would 'fly the rotor disk' instead like a conventional helicopter; it was also very stable and its sensors had a 360 degree scanning capability.

The Wideye was seriously heavy compared to its predecessors, weighing in at 275lb. It was powered by two 20hp two-stroke Weslake engines and carried a stabilized daylight television sensor. The rotor blades were initially made of wood, but were later replaced by Westland's first composite blades. The aircraft itself had an analogue computer on board (control inputs infinitely variable according to signal voltage) but its ground station was fully digital.

To save weight external electrical power was used to start the engines, but because there was no rotor brake or clutch the Wideye would start to lift off almost

as soon as the rotors began to turn, leaving no time to manually disconnect it, so the power cables were fitted with an automatic ejection system. Control of the Wideye was maintained using very narrow-band encrypted signals transmitted from a dish on the roof of the control station vehicle (now a truck rather than a Land-Rover); these signals were mated to the electronics on the air vehicle (think of an early Bluetooth work-alike!)

The Wideye progressed through several more design iterations, the next one adding a sprung undercarriage (note the clever curved legs that can be retracted into those recesses on the body just under the rotor head) and the use of more sophisticated management software and control systems

Development continued during 1977-78, with the objective of providing the UK MoD

with a demonstration on Salisbury Plain in support of a live firing exercise. Alas, the MoD began to request more and more capability enhancements (such as night vision and swarm control by a single operator) adding delay and complexity to what was intended originally to be only a proof of concept system.

This resulted in cancellation by the MoD in 1979 because of cost over-runs and delays (in fact caused by their own passion for scope-creep and yes, this still happens today, all the time). The Royal Artillery pressed on alone without MoD support, and a series of successful flight trials were completed at the RA's Lulworth Cove ranges in 1980. However, funding ran out and the project was put on ice.

The Phoenix Project – Wideye's last chance?

The final UK opportunity for these interesting remotely-piloted air vehicles arose from the MoD's PHOENIX programme, for which Westland (with a Wideye derivative turned through 90 degrees and renamed '**Sharpeye**') was down-selected along with three fixed-wing competitors.

The Westland designers put a lot of effort into tailoring the aircraft to meet the mission requirements exactly rather than submitting a blue-sky exercise in future technology. The result was a weapons system that included an integrated digital control system, three-hour endurance on station, and a 35km radius of action. Size was reduced, ground handling was simplified and the Sharpeye's support vehicles became Land Rovers again. The previously-used Weslake piston engines were replaced by a single Norton rotary-cylinder motorcycle engine, which improved fuel consumption and reduced noise and vibration.

The Westland offering won through to the fly-off, but no further. Why? Well, to protect the initiative from the possible effects of corporate politics, Westland Aerospace (on the Isle of Wight, the Hovercraft people) had offered to 'front' the project for Yeovil in exchange for a 50-50 workshare. The MoD asked Westland to commit to a firm fixed price for 120 units plus support, but when push came to shove the IoW Technical Director could not get the Westland Yeovil board to slgn off his proposal, despite the fact that they had originally supported it – perhaps this was indeed an opportunity that fell victim to internal politics after all, but we will probably never know. Hindsight is truly 20-20 vision, but it's ironic that the winners of the competition, (GEC-Marconi, with a fixed-wing airframe) picked up a contract that was eventually worth more than three times the initial bid value, and their Phoenix aircraft were to remain in service with the MoD for another 20 years.

Sharpeye's last bow – the American Opportunity

In 1990, the Martin Marietta Corporation funded Westland to build a single Sharpeye test aircraft. This was shipped to San Diego, where it flew for extended periods supporting a classified defense evaluation program. The final flights in the States were very successful, with much thought being given to piloting techniques that would result in optimal take-off and cruise profiles.

Amusingly, neither a 'real' pilot nor a radio-control model aircraft flyer proved to be the best RPH operator – instead, a design engineer who understood the theory of helicopter flight came out top of the class! The programme ran for five years but in the end another supplier was chosen by the US DoD, thus finally ending nearly 30 years of Westland involvement in RPH, although Westland's successor, Leonardo Helicopters, has shown renewed interest in recent years.

...so what does the future hold for RPHs?

Well, the future is already here! Today's RPHs are either much larger or much smaller than the Wisp and Wideye. Smaller, electrically-powered micro- and nano-copters present a near-zero airworthiness and safety risk whilst still providing the military or civilian professional with a rock-steady and easy-to-fly-camera platform costing from as little as £20 to more than £100,000, which is still a tiny fraction of the cost of a full-sized rotorcraft.

Larger, full-sized unmanned helicopters now operate in autonomous swarms moving timber from inaccessible forests to collection-points, while others are involved in offshore ship resupply, over-the-horizon early-warning for warships, crowd surveillance, counter-insurgency, mineral detection, mapping and pipeline/pylon inspections.

By going larger and adapting older full-sized helicopters for unmanned flight, good use can be made of obsolescent airframes; their design and components will already be airworthiness-approved and there will be full spares and maintenance support, so development can be focused upon the control and mission systems.

The advances in technology since the day of the Wisp and the Wideye have been staggering, with GPS and secure satellite communications being the most important. Add inbuilt intelligence controlled by incredibly powerful microprocessors, and it's now possible to pre-program a mission, allowing the RPH to take autonomous actions to avoid collisions and adverse weather and to revert to an automatic "return to base" mode if communications fail or fuel is low. Of course, this is a

technology flow-down that we are already benefitting from with our latest 2.4Ghz R/C systems for model aircraft!

Naturally, Leonardo Helicopters is also actively considering the development of unmanned full-sized helicopters, so I've included a beautiful visualization of what the future might hold, as drawn by their ace aviation artist Gary Weller. Finally, I love these three pictures of Westland technicians with dream jobs on the RPH project back in the 1970s.

The first chap is running up an unsilenced Weslake in the experimental shop and loving every minute of it!

The second shot is of the Mote on flight trials on a lovely sunny day at Ilton airfield – apparently control was lost immediately after the picture was taken, resulting in a crash that totally wrecked the rotor blades...

The third picture shows a ready-to-fly R/C JetRanger bought-in from the Digi-Hangar and adapted for use as a mule to test the Mote's control and dynamic systems – another day out for the lads. Note the sturdy transport case for the model, doubtless made-to-measure by the Woodmill – nice one, chaps!

I would like to thank the Leonardo Helicopters Engineering and Public Affairs departments for their generous help in providing pictures and background information for this article.

A Short History of RedFin Engines, or
"Q: How do you make a small fortune out of model aero-engines?"
"A: Start with a large one!"
(by Alex Phinn)

Are you sitting comfortably? Good! Now, here's a question for you: "How many modellers have dreamed of building, or even tried to build their own engines?" Well, many probably have, and some may have even have succeeded, but very few have gone on to make them in quantity. I never started out to do that - I only wanted a few for my own needs, both to satisfy my curiosity and to prove the ideas which I had nurtured for many a long year, but things actually turned out very differently!

So what's my background? I'm a semi-retired electrical engineer and company director. I was born and primarily educated in Australia, arriving in the UK as a teenager in 1956. In May 1957 I became an apprentice in the Royal Air Force; after serving for 15 years I left and took on a variety of positions in teaching and management, culminating in running my own companies.

1: Some of the' RedFin' range we'll be talking about!

I confess that I am a frustrated inventor/designer, always hankering to play with things to try and make them better (not always successfully, I hasten to add!) I've always liked the idea of designing or creating something different and I suppose that this comes down to the fact that I am an Aquarian.

Aeromodelling has always given me the outlet for my creative urges and skills, allowing me to experiment with different ideas, designs and shapes to see if there were any improvements to be made, or to just build something unusual that still flew; and although I'm formally trained in the field of electrics and electronics, my first love has always been mechanical engineering and engines – it's been with me forever and long may it remain so!

It all started one boring wet afternoon back in '09 with nothing particular to do – I was idly playing around on a 2D AutoCAD system and a shape kind of grew out of the screen which I came to recognise as being a model engine, and the more I played with it the more I began to like what was materialising. I kept returning to the idea until well into 2011 before I had settled on a layout which was both appealing and (I thought at the time) practicable.

This was based wholly on my opinion and ideas of what would constitute a good engine with reasonable performance and what it should look like. Drawing the engine was in itself very therapeutic and one could indulge in flights of fantasy; the more I did, the more I wanted to do. In the end I drew each component in detail, including every step in the imaginary process needed to make it on an virtual milling machine or lathe, starting with a block of aluminium for the crankcase and removing metal until I'd arrived at the desired shape. It sounds all pretty simple, and it is amazing just how easily you can come to believe that this really is so!

I'd somehow come into the possession of a Cox .09 crankshaft, which I viewed as a very good first step and it's why I started with a 1.5cc engine. I'd thought that this would be one of the most difficult items of an engine to manufacture – so how wrong could I be?

Every component has its own difficulties in manufacture so why pick on the crankshaft - what had it done to deserve that? I was to find out that there were many more waiting for me as I proceeded with the venture. The drawing of the intended item was the easy part, but what I'd overlooked was a small but very vital fact; what was I going to make it with or on?

Oh b**ger, I hadn't thought of that in the initial plan – the simple fact was that I didn't have any machinery, nor for that matter did I have a lot of experience of using any of it! The moral of this is very simple: 'If you're going to start from a hard place, then make it as difficult as you can', and that's exactly what I did. Incidentally, I still have the Cox 09 crankshaft and it's still waiting for the rest of the engine...

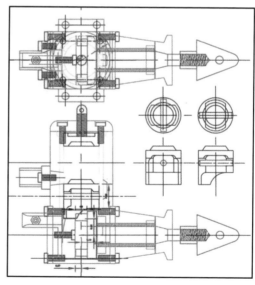

2: First experiments in CAD

Undaunted, undeterred and armed with those beautiful drawings of the components I'd created, I reasoned that I could go down to the local engineering workshop and try to negotiate their manufacture. Armed with a roll of drawings I hawked them around no less than seven machine shops both large and small in the Sheffield area and was treated to a large dose of realism in no uncertain terms. Even though these outfits were more than capable of doing such an exercise, to make 25 engines was a definite non-starter. Now if I'd asked for two and a half thousand they might have been a little more interested, and if I'd wanted twenty five thousand then it was a definite goer but of course, twenty-five thousand of my engines would be more than the entire universe would ever need!

In the course of my search I'd stumbled across a small engineering workshop near my home run by a professional tool-maker named Guy Rolf. In his workshop he'd installed several three- and four-axis computer-numerically-controlled (CNC) mills and lathes that were capable of accepting a coded programme and then machine the required shape from billet automatically. Guy had a computer programme that could do all of this but it would only work with 3D CAD drawings, and mine (of course) were 2D: oh, twice bu**er, another stumbling block!

However, Guy must have taken pity on me or maybe he simply wanted to get rid of me, so he lent me a copy of his 3D CAD package which I duly installed on my computer. I then set about learning how to use it with a will, as it seemed like fun. For the next six weeks I burned the midnight oil and eventually managed to draw the crankcase in 3D. The biggest mistake I made was trying to draw it in the same way that I'd originally envisaged making it, by starting with a cube of metal and cutting away the unwanted material – WRONG! Eventually I realised that I had to start with the smallest central object and build it up from there, in reality growing it rather than shrinking it. Once I'd cottoned on to this concept, then the rest was a stroll in a (dark) park...

3: ...looks like a crankcase!

Armed with the new 3D CAD drawings I boldly marched back into the tool shop fully expecting a miracle. Guy was somewhat shocked to see me back so soon, having most likely expected that I would be gone for months and months. Well, he was to learn that I was 'on a mission' and nothing was going to stop me achieving it!

True to his word Guy set about regenerating my CAD drawing of the crankcase so that it could be converted into 'G' code that the machine could follow to mill out the shape that I had conjured up. This translated into 29,000 lines of instruction code for the milling machine and that was only just for the top half - the internal machining would need to be done on a lathe. It took in excess of three hours of chuntering to hack out the top of the crankcase. I stood there open-mouthed, watching with awe as the shape gradually emerged from the solid piece of aluminium clamped to the machine bed.

After the first stage had been machined I saw that the programme need tweaking,

4: Taking shape in the mill

(more hours of machine time); we then made three attempts to produce the crankcase, tying up Guy's machine for more hours. I very soon realised that it was never going to be a commercial proposition and that the cost of a few of these crankcases would be stupendous...

By way of compensation for the time Guy's machines had been tied up on my project I was able to use my new-found skills in 3D CAD to do a lot of work for him. At this time I was still obsessed with the idea of machining my crankcases out of bar stock, and now understanding that this was going to take some time, I reasoned that the best way forward was for me to have my own CNC mill so as not to monopolise Guy's machines. I would also have the option in busy times of leaving work on the machine until I could get back to it. Guy was vey accommodating, saying that I could have a small corner of his shop to work in for my project.

Getting my own mill was to be the next big mistake and an expensive one at that (£6K). The machine I'd bought duly arrived and I installed it. I then had to sort out and program all the parameters for the software, including getting the relevant licence for the 'MACH 3' CAD programme that it would be running. Although I'd done some programming for microprocessors before, what I didn't have was a feel for the machine – by this I mean that I hadn't really done anything relating to the cutting of metal before and therefore I had no appreciation of tool speeds, cutting depths and rates.

5: The next big mistake!

I still have the first three attempts of milling the crankcase out bar stock - they serve to remind me of the folly of ignorance, as if I needed a reminder! The machine (a Syil X5) was eventually installed in the garage. It was time for a tactical retreat and a re-assessment of the design and where I had got to with it. I later realised that this engine was wholly impracticable, but it set me on a course that eventually led to the first of the simplified RedFin Millish engines. I also determined that I could not take a lot of very valuable production time from a good friend, so I had to become more independent and to have my own machines.

I reasoned that what I needed was an additional small manual milling machine so that I could practise before turning the big machine loose without fear that it would devour itself. I reasoned that the small mill could always be used for making one-offs or making the components for my own engine. That, as it transpired, was my next mistake...

I had little or no practical experience in machining apart from a little I did during my early apprenticeship days with the RAF, but this did not deter me; while browsing the web I found a Clarke CMD300 mill which I thought would be just the job so I bought it, complete with a digital speed readout for the spindle; I had to install that myself. All went well, and I soon started to 'make chips' with it. Of course, this wasn't the end of the milling saga as I soon outgrew it, realising after a lot of cranking the bed back and forth that there had to be an easier way – besides, it didn't have the power to cut steel, with any attempt to do so only resulting in a broken main drive gear wheel!

Having now got the ability to remove metal, what I then wanted to know was how much I'd removed - once it's gone you can't put it back! I really needed a full three-axis Digital Read-Out (DRO) machine so why hadn't I bought one in the first place? You could put it down to ignorance, but in reality it was impatience and the need to press on and get something done. In the end, with all the purchases of tools, cutters, vices and clamps I was well into big bucks but still had nothing to show for my investment - it was a good job that my chief accountant didn't know the extent of my investment!

While all of this was going on I was alternating between 2D and 3D CAD systems for my new 'Millish' design. I found that by initially drawing something in 2D, I could get all of the dimensions right, then translate that into a 3D CAD drawing and see what a design might look like in the metal. It was also good for practicing my CAD skills, in which I became reasonably proficient, but like all things if you don't keep using it, you'll soon be losing it...

6: The first small diesel prototype from CS

Eventually, after a lot of false starts, I managed to produce something that almost looked like a crankcase, but because I didn't have a lathe at that stage I was restricted in what I could do, and I still hadn't actually made a complete engine...

The action now moves to the Far East! I'd been communicating with the proprietor of CS Engines in China, Mr Gao Guo Jun, regarding the vintage replica engines he'd been manufacturing and selling. It occurred to me that here might be the opportunity that I'd been looking for, so in 2012 I asked him (with my tongue firmly in my cheek!) whether he would be interested in making a small diesel engine for me. He replied almost immediately, asking for some drawings of what I was looking for - and the rest (as they say) is history! Gao produced two prototypes for me and I had them on my bench to test within six weeks - at last, an engine I could touch!

To think that I could have avoided all of my earlier woes by going to him at the beginning! But in fact I wasn't finished yet – to satisfy myself I still needed to actually make engines with my own hands, so I went ahead and procured a lathe, the missing component from my own machine shop and essential for prototyping.

After initial testing I gave Gao the go ahead to produce a batch of 100 engines. At the time I had great reservations about this; I didn't honestly expect to sell this many and dreaded the potential loss I might incur. Having ordered the engines I then had to produce all the associated paraphernalia too, including instruction sheets, brochures and labels for the packaging. I'd been looking for suitable packaging for the engines for some time, and had discovered quite by chance that they fitted very nicely into a calling-card box which I just happened to have lying around on my office desk. I'd always had in mind that I was going to call my engine the 'REDFIN + something', hence RED was always going to feature within the name. Why should RED be so synonymous with the engine? Well, from the moment I joined the RAF many years ago I was known by the nickname 'Red Fin'!

Having sorted out a suitable box, I naturally wanted them to be red, and it just so happened that a well-known supplier could do exactly that. Those red boxes became the norm for the 049 engines; later I used different colours for different variants of the engines so as to make identification easier without having to open every box to see what was inside - pink for the 030, purple for the 061, blue for the Kompish and green for the 020. At about this time I met up with Mike Parker, who kindly did the

7: Those essential red boxes!

first review of the 'Millish 049' which appeared soon after in the March 2013 'Speaks'; this was followed by the first of the Maris Diesler reviews in the Aeromodeller magazine in Sept-Oct 2013, and very soon after this engine became and remains the biggest selling single variant.

In the meantime I'd been so busy with the marketing elements of the project that I had lost sight of the need to sell the engines! My first real foray into selling them was to turn up at Old Warden with a comfortable chair and a few boxes of engines

placed on the ground and then wait – and to my total surprise, I actually sold some!

Having made the 049 it was a very easy step to have it bored out to make it an 061 or 1.0cc, and then we just had to do a 1.5cc (.09) – in between this lot we tried making reed valve versions of the 049 and the 061, but these didn't prove to be very popular although they were the most powerful of their type.

8: Short run .030 - one of just ten

Unfortunately the indifferent quality of the engines coming through from China was becoming a problem, and I was spending anything up to an hour sorting each one out to get them to run well. On the plus side, development ideas still abounded and this kept me going. Neither had I given up on the twins - concepts like the 'Flatish' came and went, then there was the 'Tandish' for an inline twin and last of all the 'Veeish', a really terrible idea!

At this point, because of the quality issues with the engines, I started to look for an alternative manufacturer. Co-incidentally, I learnt that Gao was intending to retire and that his sons were not interested in taking over and running his business, so I immediately negotiated the purchase of all his remaining stock of engines and spare parts so that I could continue to provide ongoing support to my customers.

The story now moves quickly via the Canary Islands to the Ukraine! Engine manufacturer Alberto Parra had purchased several 09s from me to encourage some of the younger members of his club to handle i/c engines. I told him that I was looking for another engine manufacturer as Goa was going to retire, so he suggested that I should contact the man who makes his engines - Alexandr Matusha in the Ukraine; Alberto and Alexandr had gone into partnership some time earlier and he was making the Parra range of

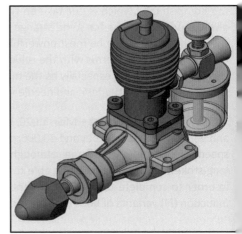

9: Alexandr's superb CAD skills

engines. These are very good quality, high performance engines so I had no problem with the idea of working with Alexandr. I sent my proposed 3D CAD drawings to him but he politely rejected them as 'rubbish' then set about redrawing them for me! It was evident that he was far more proficient with CAD software than I, being able to use it to draw and check all fits and clearances for the engines. He also suggested that a cast crankcase would turn out to be cheaper in the long run than my original machined crankcase and once again he was right - I put it down to his experience in the Russian aerospace industry prior to the breakup of the USSR.

10: One of Alex's 'Chimera' motors

To me, the most important element of this exercise was to ensure that the new engines incorporated as many of the same components as the original Chinese versions as possible, as I did not want to have two entirely different engines to support. Alexandr took this on board and did an absolutely fantastic job, with almost all parts being interchangeable with the earlier engines. To prove this point I have since made up a number of 'Chimera' engines with a Chinese bottom end and a Ukrainian top end, and they all run exceedingly well.

The batch of engines duly arrived; I bench-tested them all and I had no problems with any of them - I was very pleased indeed! Since then we've also made the Kompish 030, which is our take on the old ED MK II Comp Special - this engine always appealed to me for some strange reason, closely followed by the Millish 030 RV which turned out to be most powerful of them all, but not the most popular. I've never really come to terms with the reluctance of the modelling fraternity to accept this type of induction, especially as the main point of the engine was that it could be run inverted leaving the tank and needle valve at the top for easy access.

The next version was the Millish 020, at 0.375cc the smallest engine of this type and very high revving to beyond 20,000rpm; who would ever want to use it at those speeds is still a mystery to me, although Maris Disler was mightily impressed by a long stoke side port engine being able to run that fast when he reviewed it. Finally, in order to complete the set of different induction systems we manufactured front induction (FI) variants of both the Millish and the Kompish.

You might be asking yourself why 'Kompish' and not 'Compish'; well there was another one of those translational cock-ups! What with the delays in mailing back and forth we managed to get the marketing out of sync with the making, so the engines are cast with a 'C' while the brochure uses a 'K' just to add to the confusion! Actually, I'd thought that using 'Kompish' would make it sound and look more Eastern European, and had even considered re-naming the 'Millish' to 'Millich' for the same reason...

I continued to discuss with Alexandr my future plans for various engine types and layouts, including a multi-cylinder engine. I'd been playing around with the concept for several years and had made a few engineering mock-ups, so I had a good idea of what one might look like – I really believe that there's nothing like the Mark One eyeball to get the real feel of how it should be.

To help the project along I'd purchased some 'Boddo' spare parts from Andrew Boddington, who was unloading some of his father's kit after David's sad passing. Andrew was aware that I was considering a multi cylinder engine, as was Tom Crompton, and between us we'd come up with several prototypes which ran very well. I'd provided some sets of piston and liners for the development and had suggested using a reed valve for the induction system as this negated the problems of induction timing. The subsequent development was geared towards the making of a flat twin, which ultimately became the 'TwinFin'; because each of the earlier engine types were proven designs,

11: The 'TwinFin'

when we combined all of their features together we could be pretty confident that it was going to work and work well.

The time had now come to grasp the bull by its whatsits; we knew that we had a good working variant of the flat twin that was ultimately to become the 'TwinFin' 060, comprising of two 030 cylinders and pistons mounted in a common crankcase and crankshaft.

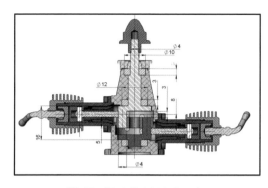

12: The 'Twinfin' CAD drawing

The original prototypes had a two-piece crankshaft, but Alexandr had decided on a three-piece crank mounted on three ball-races for the production engines. This involved some very tricky engineering, but he was happy to undertake it as a challenge. In order to achieve this, the crankshaft is made in three pieces that are welded together and finally ground between centres to ensure that everything runs square and true. As a consequence the engine has to be assembled in a jig right through to final assembly.

Having at last achieved the multi-cylinder engine that I'd been dreaming of and working on for a number of years, I took time out to look back over that achievement and wonder what to do next.

The obvious answer was to make the Millish 049 TBR SP, as I was getting very low on stock of the original Chinese variants. The resulting engine surpassed our wildest expectations with regards to performance and handling and is possibly a little too powerful. "Any chance of more power?" you might ask. Oh yes - enter the TwinFin 099, producing 0.17bhp at 15,000rpm – would that be

enough for you, sir? It's the one of the newest addition to the range of RedFin engines and comprises of two 049's, and still adheres to our time-honoured tradition of using common components from other engines to make the next one.

Is this the end of the RedFin Range of engines? Well, actually, no! Following discussions and some friendly pressure from the SAM35 Committee, I agreed to produce a limited run of special 'SAM .35' and 'SAM .50' engines for sale to the membership. It's intended to run events especially for these engines and a new model design has been commissioned to suit them – it will be available soon - and 'SAM .35' engine number 35 will be offered as a prize in one of these events!

To obtain one or both of these motors (£110 each or £200 plus P&P for both as a special offer to SAM35 members only), please contact Kevin Richards, Old Bear Barn, 19 Ebor Court, Northallerton, North Yorkshire, DL7 8RY. Tel: 01609 772818. Email: kevin.richards2@tiscali.co.uk.

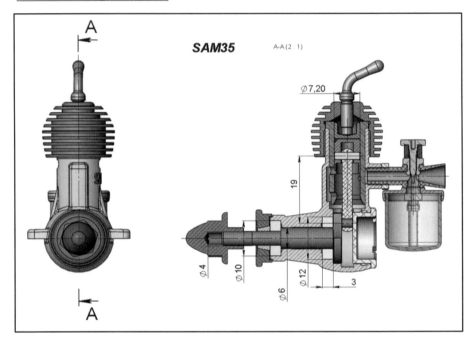

When I started out I thought that I knew a little about model engines, and in particular about model diesel engines. As this development has gone on I've realised just how little it was that I knew, and if I had been honest with myself then I would never have set out on this long, tortuous and very expensive path, It has left me thinking of others who, like me, who have been using little diesel engines for many years and think that they know a little about them. How right they are, they know a very little about them!

Every engine is different and you have to get to know the idiosyncrasies of each; what applies to one may not necessarily apply to another, and this is especially true when we are talking about twins as they are an altogether different beast! I've come to the conclusion that the more I know about engines, the more there is that I don't know about them, and maybe life is too short to fathom this bottomless pit...

Finally, would I do it all again? Yes, but next time I would start ten years earlier!

REDFIN Engine Sales: Snapshot taken in early 2018					
Chinese	**Made**	**Sold**	**Ukrainian**	**Made**	**Sold**
049 PB SP	230	215	030 TBR SP	206	180
030 PB SP	200	195	030 TBR KOMP	134	134
061 PB SP	100	98	030 TBR RV	111	69
090 PB SP	100	98	020 TBR SP	105	105
049 PB RV	100	43	030 TBR FI	106	92
061 PB RV	100	35	030 TBR KFI	99	49
			020 TBR KOMP	99	49
			060 TBR Twin	169	134
			049 TBR SP	99	55
			099TBR Twin	52	32
Totals:	**830**	**684**	**Totals:**	**1180**	**899**

Acknowledgements:

Gou Goa Jun: The essential first step on a long path
Alexandr Matusha: Whose skill and knowledge has made this all possible
Tom Crompton: Mentor and confidante - without his encouragement this adventure would never have been possible
Mike Parker: Always a great help and critic
Ted Smails: Master 'cranker', first to start the RF 049 PB SP
Guy Rolf: Master tool maker, his help and encouragement has been indispensable
Kevin Richards: A very knowledgeable sounding board!

...and to all my loyal clients who, by purchasing my engines, have each contributed in their own individual way to make this journey an exciting and very interesting one!

SAM .35 (left) and SAM .50 (right)

Designing, trimming and flying an all-purpose Soarer -
'FINGER PROBE' *(by Gordon 'Gamma' Rae)*

"A big simple thermal and light-wind two-channel soarer, capable of being loaded up for rougher conditions and with good responsive handling, that's what we want, Gordon!" demanded the magazine editor...

"Is that all?" I mused, at this request - some people are never satisfied! Nevertheless, I secretly relished the exercise, as the various characteristics required from such a glider had been popping up in the 'mixing pot' of my mind from time to time and here was an opportunity to put it all together. I'd long thought that a low aspect ratio wing, with its nice big chord encouraging higher Reynolds numbers, would provide both the manoeuverability and efficiency needed at the necessarily lower speeds required to exploit the smaller, lighter areas of thermal- and contour-induced lift.

Also required was a wing section that would fulfill these requirements while still having the ability to 'move out' when loaded to cope with winds, as well as being able to survive the inevitable rough landings to which the Malvern slopes subject a model (or is it just me?), whilst also standing up to the loads imposed by our faster tow-line sprinters.

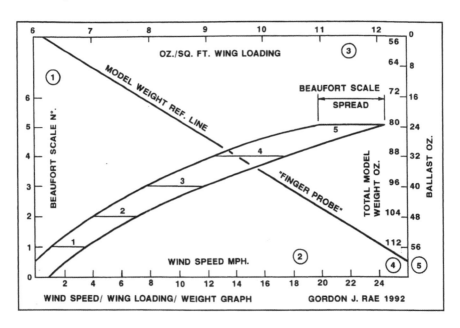

Design Considerations

The whole structure had to be up to scratch strength-wise, consistent with an unbalanced wing loading of around 6 to 7oz/sq. ft. and upwards. So, the low aspect ratio wing planform developed on my earlier 'Finger Vee' was used as a starting point to help realise these requirements. To contribute to handling, the polar moments of the airframe are kept low, with a shortish nose and light wing and tail extremities. For efficiency at high angles of attack, curved low drag vortex shedding tips are used on the wings.

In order to promote a reasonably high Re at the lower wing loadings, the generous wing chord was planned to give, at its lower speed of 12.5 mph (18.4 fps), an Re of around 130k, going up to Re 200k at the upper end of the level flight speed range of 22 mph (32.2 fps). There should also be a satisfactory increase in these figures as the wing loading goes up.

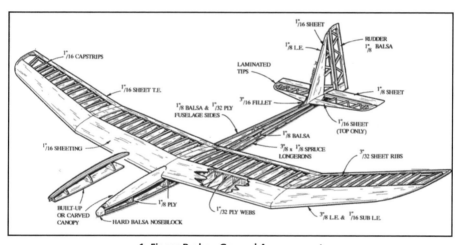

1: Finger Probe - General Arrangement

The outcome of analysing and reconciling all these requirements eventually led me to the design shown above – the 'Finger Probe'. Its 'Rhode St Genese 29' wing section is well suited to the expected velocity regime, and although a bit on the light side at its un-ballasted wing loading of around 6 to 7oz sq. ft. the 'Probe' floats around nicely at this weight. The optimum loading is about 8oz/sq. ft, going up to a maximum of something like 10oz/sq. ft. At these high wing loadings with a required all-up weight approaching 6lbs, it's pushing the standard wing structure towards its upper limit (see graph) if it is subjected to extreme loads.

For serious competition flying at these loadings, particularly when steep, fast F3B ping-type launches are indulged in, carbon-fibre tows can usefully be added to the spar or the sheeting extended over the total centre wing surface and glassed over with light-weight skinning. One could also use top surface spoilers.

However, I rather like the simpler version without these 'competition extras' and in this form she flies beautifully. On the slope the standard 'Probe' will cope with winds of 10 to 15 mph at the 8oz/sq. ft. loading level and although it will fly in stronger winds, one would be operating at the upper end of its drag range and penetration could be the final limiting factor. The accompanying weight/loading graph will simplify the choice of correct model weight for a given wing loading as dictated by the flying conditions.

Trimming the Model:

The figures and suggestions below are optimised for the 'Probe', but should also prove to be a handy guide for builders of other soaring gliders. If you like playing these sort of games and have decided, with the aid of the graph above what weight you are going to use, it should be added to the under-wing space at the centre of gravity. The ballast can conveniently be carried as lead pieces in small plastic bags, securely strapped in place with rubber bands over the hooks provided. Most dynamic machines benefit from fine tuning and a soarer is no exception. Initial flights with the Probe showed a small 'excess of stability' (appreciated by some pilots) which manifests itself in Probe's reluctance to spiral dive or spin if any up elevator trim is used. She just settles into a tight circling flight with very little loss of height. Great for thermal flying at long range, but not much use for losing height, which a spiral dive will do without putting too much strain on things.

A little adjustment was deemed necessary; it needed a tiny rearward shift of the Centre of Lateral Area (CLA). As I didn't want to mess around with my lovely fin, the other course of action was taken, that is to reduce the dihedral of the wings slightly. This, together with an increase of outer panel leading edge sweep to compensate, had the desired effect whilst still maintaining the excellent low speed handling. Probe loved it and will now, if provoked, drop her nose and rotate, and also benefits from a marginally flatter glide, together with a slight increase in sensitivity to thermal disturbances (observed) - not a bad return for a bit of 'frigging with the rigging'!

I like my models to last, and in fact I still fly quite regularly my 'Finger One' glider that was constructed in 1974. This is a very useful and much used model, so much that the airframe, in places, has succumbed to fatigue which shows up as cracks in the airframe and gives a very good indication where the high stress points are.

Probing the Atmosphere:

If you have built your model accurately and free from warps (apart from just a trace of washout at each tip) the first flight will be a doddle. Balance at the wing root at the optimum starting point, (for the Probe, this is 4¼" back from wing leading edge), and with the rudder, elevator, and transmitter trims in their neutral position, and operating in the correct sense, you are all set to go. A straight horizontal launch out from the slope in a light wind will have the model climbing up and away. Towline launch is just as easy; the Probe will go up the line with perhaps just a touch of rudder to keep it tracking straight.

A little up trim on subsequent line launches will gain that extra height to grab those thermals. Small control inputs are the 'order of the day' for thermal seeking. Fly forward if there is an appreciable wind and look for those tell-tale indicators of lift, like thermalling raptors, or swifts having their thermal-borne insect lunch. Watch closely for a change of height or a lifted wing which are sure indicators of lift.

Initial trimming: Positive Pitch

Gain some height, position into wind and put her into a shallow dive say 20 degrees or level flight, somewhat faster than normal, return the Tx stick to neutral, and observe. On neutralising the Tx stick your aircraft should start to climb with the speed slowly decaying and, if no control is used, will eventually go up into a gentle stall. You can level out just before the stall if you wish. If the climb is quite steep, this indicates a definite 'positive pitch' response and is more than we require for optimum, level flight performance. Land and remove some nose weight to shift the balance point back ¼", then fly the test pattern again and repeat if necessary until the flight pattern is correct.

As you have now flown with the balance point at the front of its range, now is also a good time to try shifting it back a little and in so doing reduce, by a small amount, the down load on the tail, the angle of attack and subsequently the induced drag of the wing. All will have collectively small beneficial effects on performances. Choose light wind conditions (onto slope face) and fly your model to check that it does, in fact, fly straight and level with its elevator trims in neutral. If not, adjust balance until correct.

Initial trimming: Negative Pitch

You may go a bit too far with the rearward movement of the balance point. If you reach this situation, your model, when pulled out from its dive and stabilised into level flight, will, on neutralising the Tx stick, start to increase speed again and go into a progressively increasing dive. This is very definitely 'negative pitch response', and is positively a no-no for our required control response. Although I like to set up my aerobatic slopers this way, it can be a little extreme for a thermal machine.

Interestingly, with a just negative pitch response trim, you will find that at normal level flight speed your aircraft will fly quite happily along in level flight. It's only when it is 'speeded up' that the dive syndrome takes over. The remedy is simply to replace a small amount of nose weight to restore sufficient positive pitch stability. It is possible to put in some practice useful for thermalling on your local slope.

Initial trimming: Optimisation

After the initial excitement of the 'first flights' has been overcome, you should settle down to checking for optimum performance. This can be done off the line, but is more conveniently flown from the slope. With all trims in neutral, put the model into a reasonable perceptible climb and if left to continue it should finally resume level flight without help from the intrepid pilot. Choose a light breeze on to the slope and cruise back and forth along the front of the slope, turning out and forward at each end of your beat. Practice your turns using combinations of rudder and elevator. The aim is to eliminate any pitch oscillations. Keep the height constant, don't climb into the turn or dive out of it. Keep it level. When you can fly accurately in this way you will be able to exploit small pockets of 'lift opportunity', either using "Yank and Bank" or 'Cajole and Suggest' tactics to perform mild aerobatics or to merely cruise back and forth along the slope in next-to-nothing of lift.

Whether you decide to build a 'Probe' as your next soarer, or choose another design, I believe that this article will give you the information you need to be successful in trimming and flying it. Of course I hope you do decide to build a Probe – if so, it will delight you with its predictable handling, making it suitable for the beginner or experienced flyers alike.

So 'go for it', have fun and good luck with your new glider! The plan for the 'Finger Probe' is available to order online from: http://www.model-plans.co.uk/rc gliders.htm

2: Gordon on the slope with 'Finger Probe'

Man-Powered Flight and the Omega Wing
The Story of a Very British Glorious Failure! *(by Jeff Fellows)*

The dream of Human-Powered Flight dates back to the classical Greek myths of Icarus and Daedalus. Over the centuries numerous efforts have been made to realise this dream, but all met with varying degrees of failure.

However, in 1959 the intervention by Henry Kremer (see picture) galvanised the whole scene. He was born in Latvia in 1907 and moved to Britain after WW1. By the time WW2 broke out he held a number of patents including those for the plywood processes used to build the De Havilland Mosquito. In 1959 he offered a prize of £5000 for the construction and flight of a machine, powered by human effort alone, that could take off and fly a figure of eight course around marks half a mile apart, starting and finishing at a height of at least 10 feet.

The competition was to be administered by the Royal Aeronautical Society and was at first limited to British-built aircraft. Across the aeronautical community there was widespread enthusiasm, and several groups began design and construction. The

1: SUMPAC – flew 650m in 1961

first to fly was the Southampton University Man Powered Aircraft (SUMPAC) built by postgraduate students from conventional materials – balsa, ply and fabric, with a minimum of metal. On 9th November 1961 SUMPAC took off from the runway at Lasham, piloted by Derek Piggot, flew and landed successfully. The best flight achieved, from forty attempts, covered 650 metres.

One week later, on 16th November, Puffin, built at the works of the De Havilland Company and piloted by John Wimpenny, flew successfully at Hatfield.

Puffin improved on the distance achieved by SUMPAC with a straight line flight of 908 metres, a record that stood for ten years. The power available from human effort and the technology then available meant that flight was only just possible; both Puffin and SUMPAC could manage sustained flight only in Ground Effect (GE), where the presence of the ground-plane reduces the power required. The benefit of ground effect is a function of the wingspan; it is greatest very near the ground but becomes negligible at heights above about half a wingspan.

Unfortunately, the need to fly in GE brings with it the problem of pitch instability. As the aircraft nears the ground, the presence of the ground-plane reduces the downwash from the wings. With a conventional configuration (tailplane behind the wing) the result is an effective increase in tailplane incidence and hence a nose down pitch, which the pilot has to correct. For SUMPAC and Puffin, both of which had low inertia in pitch, this instability was significant.

2: De Havilland's Puffin flew 900m

The Birth of the Omega Wing Concept

In 1964, when working in the Weapons Department at R.A.E. Farnborough, I was joined by John Stone, an aerodynamicist who had worked in the wind tunnels at Hatfield and had first-hand experience of Puffin. We discussed the pitch instability problem and its implications. John's belief was that the pilot's workload in controlling pitch detracted from the effort he could put into pedalling, and other studies indeed supported that conclusion.

Clearly, if an aircraft configuration could be designed that was inherently stable in pitch when in GE then the pilot could concentrate more of his effort on propulsion, so we began to search for configurations that might achieve this objective. Two designs seemed promising - one was a canard, because we believed with this arrangement, the downwash changes from the small fore-plane in GE would have less influence on stability.

The second was very radical. John suggested that we could make GE work for us to promote stability by positioning a tailplane in the upward going part of each wing tip vortex. This design involved two booms extending backwards from the wingtips. At the ends of each boom a tailplane would be positioned outboard of the wingtip. The theory was that as the aircraft descended towards the ground, the strength of the wingtip vortex would decrease, thus the effective tailplane incidence would reduce, giving a nose up pitching moment – unfortunately, at that stage we didn't think too much about the structural implications - big mistake!

Testing the Theories

However, all this was very hypothetical so we needed to establish whether our ideas would work in practice. We built a number of test models intended for indoor flying, each model being about five feet in span and eight ounces in weight with balsa and tissue construction. In each model, Venner silver-zinc accumulators of 3 volts and 1.5 amp hour capacity supplied power to a Micromax T0-3 motor geared 15 to 1, driving a 12 inch diameter balsa prop. Current consumption was less than one amp so we had consistent and uniform power throughout the tests. The models were:

1. A Short Moment Arm (SMA) conventional design similar to Puffin and SUMPAC to establish whether instability in GE was indeed a real phenomenon.	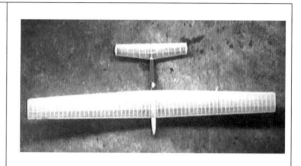
2. A similar, but Longer Moment Arm (LMA) design to establish whether putting the tailplane further back would reduce the instability.	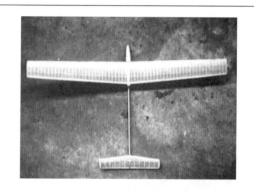
3. The new radical design, which we christened the Omega wing, for obvious reasons	

4. The same Omega model but with the tailplanes turned inboard. We thought this might result in neutral or slightly negative stability in Ground Effect.	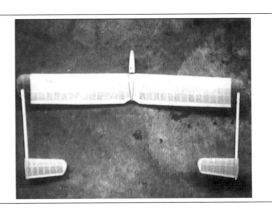

The number five model, a canard, was built but quickly discarded; it incorporated some additional ideas such as a much thicker wing section, but we struggled to make it light enough. Neither of us had much experience with canards and we never managed to make it fly properly so we abandoned it - second big mistake - especially in the light of later events!

Trials Programme #1 - Indoors

The flight trials of the four remaining models were carried out at Cardington, which was then an Royal Aircraft Establishment (R.A.E) out-station. All were free flight (no R/C) and were filmed, and the monochrome pictures in this article have been extracted from those films and included despite their low resolution as they are the only visual records left of this fascinating venture.

Each model in turn was initially trimmed to fly clear of GE to demonstrate its free flight stability. It was then trimmed to fly on a descending path into GE, and different amounts of nose down trim were used in sequential flights to see how significant the influence (If any) of Ground Effect might be.

Amazingly, the flights followed the pattern predicted! The conventional models all pitched nose down as they neared the ground, the short moment arm version more severely than the one with the longer moment arm.

The model with the tailplanes inboard showed neutral characteristics with possibly a slight but not very marked nose down pitch as it neared the ground.

However, as the Omega wing model descended into GE it levelled out and then flew at a more or less constant altitude. This altitude was dependent on the amount of nose-down pitch; with an excessively nose heavy trim it would fly just above the floor surface; with decreasing nose-down trim it would stabilise at higher and higher levels up to 2 to 3 feet.

Conclusions from the Small Model Tests

It was clear that in the Omega Wing we had a design, which, if it could be translated into full scale, would solve the pitch instability problem, would enable the aircraft to automatically follow the ground surface at a height at which the power required to maintain flight would be usefully reduced, and would allow the pilot to apply his entire effort to propulsion. On the basis of our film evidence we were given permission to build a larger model of the Omega Wing in an unused lab at the R.A.E and to carry out trials on the airfield.

3: Big Omega ready for outdoor testing

On completion, this larger model was 15 feet in span, weighed 7½ pounds and was again of conventional balsa and tissue construction. Our calculations indicated that an 0.5cc Albon Dart, driving a 6x4 inch prop, would provide just enough power to sustain level flight in Ground Effect.

Working in the evenings we completed the model just as a spell of fine and very calm weather arrived - the colour photo shows the model outside the lab in which it was built.

Trials Programme #2 - Outdoors

Transport to the main runway was via John's VW Beetle, with me sitting on the bonnet holding the model, having previously checked with Air Traffic Control that all full-sized flying had ceased. This worked well, except that on one occasion as we approached the runway the access control lights turned red. John braked, I slid off

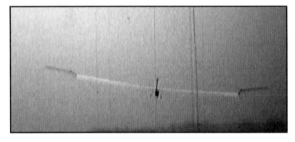

the bonnet and landed in a heap on the grass, while the model floated away and landed smoothly; soon afterwards, a light aircraft landed just ahead of us, but luckily no harm was done to either aircraft!

We flew the model on a number of evenings when it was sufficiently calm, and there were several filming sessions, and on one occasion two members of the Aero Department witnessed the trials.

The flights were successful and showed the same stability in Ground Effect that we had seen indoors with the small model, though the heights were greater because the wingspan was much larger. The

flight path followed the contours of the ground quite well, provided that the gradients were not too steep.

Once again we found that a very nose down trim resulted in a flight near to the ground and that reducing the down trim led to increases in altitude. The power available however was insufficient to fly outside ground effect, so that too much up trim resulted in a non-divergent phugoid type of flight at a lower altitude.

The Death of the Omega Project

Although we had proved the concept, we had two problems that turned out to be insurmountable in respect of taking the trials further. The first was structural; even at 15 feet span the conventional materials and structure were not up to the job, and like Puffin and SUMPAC, warps set in. The aero-elastic problems caused by hanging long booms and tailplanes on the ends of the wings were also serious; when we later added radio control and ailerons we found that although the model would turn, the direction of turn was always opposite to that commanded! It was clear that we could not simply scale up the model and have any chance of success. Perhaps, with the materials available today it might just be possible, but not in 1964!

These problems, together with the opposition of some senior members within the Aero Department, who felt that two junior upstarts from Weapons Department should not be meddling in aircraft matters, eventually brought the project to a close. It was therefore a classical VBGF (Very British Glorious Failure) and great fun while it lasted, but that wasn't quite the end of the story…

Enter Uncle Sam…

In 1973, the Kremer prize was increased to £50,000 and eligibility widened from "British Only" to worldwide, which of course included America.

By 1977 there were some 20 projects underway in several countries. The first man-powered flight in the USA was in April 1976, and in August 1977 the first Kremer Prize was won by Gossamer Condor, which flew the figure of eight course covering 2172 metres.

The design, by Dr Paul MacCready and Dr Peter Lissaman was a canard, the configuration that John and I had identified as an option but failed to translate into a satisfactory model for our trials 13 years previously. The use of modern materials resulted in a structural weight for Gossamer Condor of only 30kg, roughly half that of Puffin and SUMPAC.

4: Gossamer Condor

5: Gossamer Albatross

The large wing area and hence low wing loading allowed a relatively low flying speed by comparison with those earlier designs, and bracing wires (which at low speeds contribute little drag) could now be used to maintain the structural integrity. Most importantly, low speed meant that less power was required to maintain flight. Sustained human powered flight was now a reality. In June 1979 Gossamer Albatross, another canard, won a Kramer prize for crossing the English Channel, and by April 1988 designs had improved so dramatically that the MIT Aeronautics Department's Daedalus was able to fly from Crete to the island of Santorini, a distance of 71.5 miles, in 3 hours 54 minutes, a record that still stands to this day.

Acknowledgement: I'm indebted to John Stone who provided a great deal of the material used in this article and was responsible for the Omega Wing concept itself – and he also carved the superb balsa props used on the small trials models – thank you, John!

THE QI's HOT TIPS #2: Running-in Electric Motors Underwater!

It may sound strange, but the best way to bed in the parts of an electric motor that rub against each other is to fill a plastic tub with clean water, suspend the motor from a wooden or plastic spar, connect it up to a battery and let it run for half an hour then stop, wash it out, refill the bowl and do it again.

After the second run, dry it off and lubricate the bearings with 3-in-1 or a similar oil and you're good to go. Running underwater is good because it minimises arcing and pitting and catches the debris generated by mating the parts.

Oh, just one thing – I meant to say that you MUSTN'T do this with brushless motors! No, no, please stop, DON'T put that ESC and RX under water! Don't… Oh dear, too late! Never mind, that'll be some more business for Hobby King then, and another non-conformance report for me to write up…

MODELLING WITH CARBON FIBRE
A High-Tech material produced using Low-Tech methods!
(by Bill Longley)

First of all, what is carbon fibre? Well, it looks like black string made from multiple strands called 'tows'. This 'string' comes in different sizes classified by the number of filaments or strands making up the tow. So, '12k' means that there are 12,000 filaments per tow and 3K means there are 3000. Each carbon filament in the tow is a continuous cylinder with a diameter of 5–8 micrometers and consists almost exclusively of carbon. Carbon fibre (CF) can be woven to make cloth of differing weights and thicknesses depending upon the tow used. Most common is 200 grams/sq.metre, which is made of 3k tow – a single layer is approximately 0.2 mms thick.

You've probably heard the expression 'pre-preg' in relation to CF - this is simply carbon cloth which is manufactured with resin already encompassing ('impregnating') the fibres. Without resin, the cloth has no strength and cannot be used to make parts or finish models. The resin in the pre-preg cloth will still be slightly sticky but not runny, and will require heat (120- 220 degrees C) over several hours to fully cure. For full benefit the material should be moulded in an autoclave, which not only gives the necessary heat but also pressurises the material at up to 5 atmospheres.

The main advantage of using pre-preg cloth is that the process does not require skilled workers, saving on labour and re-work costs. Why? Well, the cloth is easy to cut to a pattern, the material keeps its shape and does not fray at the edges, and the resulting mouldings cannot be bettered, thus explaining why Airbus, Boeing and all other major aerospace manufacturers use it.

However, there is a down-side for industrial users in terms of plant and material costs, which are extremely high. Pre-preg cloth is triple the price of cloth and resin separately, you will need moulds made by a skilled person to get the best results, and even a small autoclave will set you back upwards of £250,000. Also, damage to CF objects usually results in replacement rather than repair, due to broken fibres robbing the item of its inherent strength.

However, CF is light, strong, rigid and fatigue-resistant, so what can aeromodellers use it for, and how can we achieve the best results on the bench in our man-caves? Well, the flat sheet makes very good control horns, engine mountings, structural parts and even complete aeroplanes (see picture on page 122). CF is easily worked, and can be cut, filed, and drilled with ordinary hand tools.

So, first and foremost, we need to remember that we're probably going to be dealing with smaller and much thinner moulded items than Airbus or McClaren, so by clamping flat sheets between pieces of Contiboard or metal angle strip, high surface pressures can easily be attained. The usual reason for advising against simple hand lay-up is the skill required to achieve the correct cloth-to-resin ratio, but with the method I describe below this is not an issue. Excess resin is applied in the lay-up then, when under pressure, any excess is squeezed out leaving an optimum laminate in the process.

I use 'peel-ply' which gives an excellent bonding surface; it's a nylon or polyester cloth impregnated with PTFE most commonly used to create a textured surface on a laminate, and is ideal for secondary laminating and bonding. Being a porous layer, peel-ply allows the bleeding of trapped air and helps to minimise any excess resin in the laminate. The carbon cloth used is 200g plain weave.

When working with epoxy resin, cleanliness is paramount! The usual advice given is to wear gloves, but I do not - if I do get resin on my fingers, I immediately clean it off. In all my years of experience, I have found that employees who wear gloves are the worst contaminators because they're unaware that they have resin on their gloves, so this is then passed onto all the tools they're using, the mould, the bench, everywhere! Whether you choose gloves or not, it's imperative that you never touch any wet resin – move the laminates with the brush, never your fingers!

(MM: to see the build of an F2B Stunter made almost completely from CF, this link is well worth looking at: http://controlline.org.uk/phpBB2/viewtopic.php?t=14375)

A: This shows the preparation of materials, with four or two layers of laminate, a pair of sheets of release film, a sheet of peel ply, and the clamping boards/aluminium angle	
B: Commencement of wetting out; lay the first layer on the first release film, apply resin with the brush, applying layers individually **NEVER touch with fingers anything that is wet with resin!**	
C: Wet out very thoroughly; any excess resin is squeezed out later	
D: Apply the peel-ply, wet through and you will be able to squeeze out any air bubbles	

E: Having placed the second release film on top, now clamp the sandwich between the boards and/or angles, using all the clamps you've got, and more!

F: Here's the clamping of the flat piece...

G: After 24 hours curing, un-clamp and separate from the release films

H: The peel-ply is harder to remove, but here shows the bonding surface

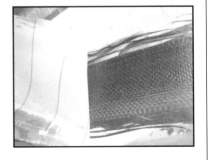

J: the comparative finish, showing peel-ply against the release film	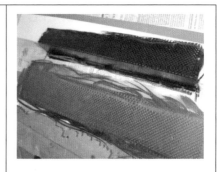
K: The finished articles: four layers (flat) is 0.6mm thick; two layers (angle) is 0.4mm thick	

I say, Eve, one of my ribs is missing!

WEATHERMAN C/L SPEED – how to be a Winner!
(by Tony Goodger)

Why Weatherman?

If you're like me, your first experience of aeromodelling many years ago was control line. R/C was in its infancy and anyway far too expensive to finance on my

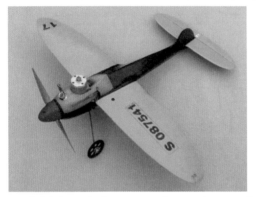

meagre pocket money. Having slowly graduated into competing, albeit with little success, I was distracted by other interests and bringing up a family, but I never lost my early fascination with those lines and that handle...

Looking at modern C/L speed flying, the thought of trying to take part competitively must be rather daunting - most classes require very specialist knowledge, expensive engines and lots of practice. With this in mind, SAM35's Dick Roberts and Brian Lever had the brilliant idea of starting a new speed class based upon the 1949 'Weatherman' design by Cyril Shaw.

It's a relatively simple model with a fixed two-wheel undercarriage, long moment arm giving excellent flying characteristics and originally designed to be powered by a Mills 1.3 diesel engine. By allowing an unlimited choice of engines within several distinct classes, using only fuel allowed by the BMFA rules, restricting the engine to suction feed and not allowing exhaust extensions or tuned exhaust systems, a large choice became available. This allowed older engines designed for open exhausts to compete effectively with more modern engines.

As the original classes have now inevitably become very competitive, we've recently introduced a new profile class with a limited engine choice aimed at beginners; my design for this model was published in the April 2015 Aeromodeller, together with building instructions. It's called 'Clubman Profile Weatherman' and competitors are split into novice and expert classes.

Weatherman speed in all its forms has now become very popular around the world proving the viability of the concept, so why not come and join us for some relaxed fun sport or competition flying? This article is intended to give you all the information you need to build and fly a 'Weatherman' model successfully.

Rules

The first step when considering flying in any of the original Weatherman classes is to study the rules, which are available on both the BMFA and SAM35 web sites. The Profile Weatherman rules are on the SAM35 site only – follow this link to download either: http://sam35.org.uk/rules/

Plans

The next step is to study the plan. The original isn't generally available so I've redrawn it to include details of strengthening to accommodate more powerful engines and a suggested tank design *(shown at the end of this article)*. Although no material sizes are shown, these can be measured from the plan, of which copies are readily available. Note that for the 1.0cc class, the plan is reduced by a factor of 25% to give a wing span of 14" and for the 6.6cc and 10cc classes the plan is increased by a factor of 1.414 to give a minimum span of 26.6".

Engine

Before beginning construction, the modeller needs to decide which class to enter and what engine to use. Engine choice is virtually unlimited. My suggestion is that you start with an engine you know, then see what others use and move on from there. Some records are held by engines dating back to the 1980s and before; I once held the Class 6 record using a K&B rat race engine purchased at a swapmeet for £5!

To obtain maximum engine performance it will almost certainly be necessary to make a new venturi (either a complete air intake or a restrictor). When running an engine on suction, a peripheral-type venturi will not allow maximum performance to be obtained. The objective is to obtain a clean takeoff without the engine cutting out – you'll find that engines that run satisfactorily on the ground with a very large venturi will not work in the air! I use an OS-style single-jet needle valve assembly with the outlet positioned in the centre of the airflow and its end bevelled off.

Fuel Tank

Everybody has their own ideas on tanks and for optimum performance this will probably have to be custom made. The design shown on the plan is for a uniflow type which works for me, but some prefer front-feed tanks.

The table below gives some suggested typical data starting points for each class:

Class	Capacity cc	Venturi Bore	Prop Size	Tank cc
0	1.0			
1	Mills 1.3	Standard	7x6	
2	1.66			
3	2.5		7x4 – 7x6	6.0 Diesel - 12.0 Glow
4	3.5	6.5	7x6 – 8x6	12
5	5.0	7.0	8x7 – 9x6	15
6	6.6	7.5	9x7	20
7	10	8.0	10x7	30

Propellers

Most competitors use APC props which give a good performance. For ultimate speed you'll need to use carbon-fibre products but these do require time-consuming preparation with a pitch gauge and balancer.

Model Construction

Most of you reading this article will be competent builders so I'll only discuss special points relating to the construction. As speed timing is from a standing start this is primarily an acceleration event, so model weight is very important.

Having said that, going from a Mills 1.3 to a racing .60 engine does require modifications to strengthen the airframe, and of course the fuselage will need modifying to suit different engines both in terms of its width and frontal length.

Building the Fuselage

Prior to starting to build the fuselage, you must calculate what length it needs to be in front of the wing's leading edge to give an acceptable CG for the chosen engine (this might require a move of up to 25mm to the rear compared with the standard airframe). This can be done by a simple calculation based upon the weight and position of the original Mills 1.3. Heavier engines, particularly those with rear induction, pose issues with the model construction. As a guide, the following table gives typical dimensions recommended for the distance from the leading edge to the nose (discounting the spinner):

Class	Engine Capacity cc	Model Weight grams	Engine Weight grams	Nose Length mm
0	1.00	170	50	60
1	Mills 1.3			75
2	1.66	350	115	
3	2.50	450	150	
4	3.50	600	240	75
5	5.00	650	270	70
6	6.60	800	320	110
7	10.0	900	550	95

I always like to make my tanks removable and adjustable in position, which can mean breaking into the leading edge area. My approach is to have the bellcrank spar on the inboard wing only and introduce an additional hardwood spar, approximately one-third to one-half span, at the rear of the tank position. Note that the bellcrank has been moved forward from the original plan position. It's important that the wing is tied to the bearers with hold-downs or bolts for strength - details are shown on the updated plan.

I always mount the engine on steel or dural plates screwed and bonded to the bearers. This adds to the rigidity of mounting the engine and improves performance by reducing vibration. A half cowl will significantly reduce drag. I used to carve these from hard balsa but now use jelutong, a low density fine grain hardwood which is commonly used for carving and pattern making in the UK - alternatives are lime and basswood.

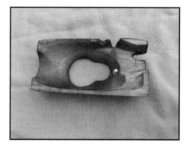

Building the Wing

The wing section shown on the original plan is a flat bottomed, lifting section which may be fine for the Mills engine, but in my opinion is unsuitable for high performance. This section risks a wing over on take-off and consequent disqualification for high flying. Whilst not really in the spirit of the rules, many builders eliminate the dihedral to give a stronger wing and make it easier to finish the wing section.

It is important to select some light, rigid balsa for the wing but with the elliptical shape using quarter grain is not essential. I always use a semi-symmetrical lifting section thinning to a symmetrical section at the tip. Some use a forward high point while some have this further back as much as 50%. I keep to typical speed model wing sections with the maximum thickness at 25/30%.

For longevity, the leading and trailing edges need to be reinforced with hardwood. The method I now use is to groove the wing blank to a depth of 6mm with a small slitting saw (1.5mm thick) mounted in a pillar drill and glue shaped plywood strips into the resulting slots. Not only does this provide the required strength, it also provides a guide for shaping the wing section. Tip weight needs to be added to prevent turning in of takeoff and as a guide I use between 10 and 50 grams depending on the size of model.

The lead-out guide holes take a lot of wear. Plywood or printed circuit board can be used but it is essential to bush the holes with brass tube or eyelets to prevent wear, and I always use a series of holes to allow adjustment before flying. The lead-out wires need to be made from 20g piano wire or heavy duty stranded wire; alternatively line connectors can be used on the bellcrank - look for 'fishing snaps' on eBay for a wide selection of sizes. Again, even if using reinforced plastics, all holes must be bushed to prevent wear.

Building the Tailplane

The tailplane/elevator is made in a similar way to the wing with a lifting section. Whilst the elevator horn is shown mounted on the underside on the plan, experience has shown that this makes them prone to damage so mounting on the top is preferable. For the larger size of model the pushrod can be made from carbon-fibre tube fitted with secure ends (also epoxy the tubes on the outside) and a midway guide to prevent bending and resonance. As the rudder is often used as a steady prior to release it needs to be strong - a centre core of 1.5mm plywood will give the required strength and there is no need to incorporate rudder offset.

Building the Undercarriage

The undercarriage needs to be strong and larger models would benefit from additional struts where it is attached to the bearers. I always have trouble bending piano-wire undercarriages accurately so use the following method. Start by cutting the specified gauge of wire to the required length with a little to spare. Then mark the bend points with a felt tip pen and bend each angle starting from the centre taking care to allow for any slippage with the bending tool and obtaining the correct orientation of bend. Wheels need to be fitted very securely and I always use a soldered washer on the inside and a collet with Loctite on the outside with the grub screw set into a groove. Suitable wheels can be difficult to obtain but if you can't make them yourself there are specialist suppliers around.

Finishing the Model

When it was first designed the model would have been finished with tissue and dope. For modern competition use I prefer to use an epoxy/glass cloth finishing system over the entire model. Properly applied this will give an immense increase in strength and durability for very little weight gain. There is plenty of information on the internet about the correct technique to use and a variety of excellent materials are available.

Flying the Model

All control-line ends should be made up in accordance with BMFA Speed model rules. Beware of some makes of stranded stainless steel wire that are available – it can be much weaker than single-strand spring steel wire of the same size.

This is an excellent flying model provided it is built according to the plan and the CG is in the recommended position. Experience and testing has shown that the model can be flown easily by a novice pilot. We have also flown them in very strong winds without a problem (even the Mills-powered version!) provided that it's kept low on take-off. The rules allow whipping of the model only on the first lap, which can greatly improve the final speed. However care must be exercised to maintain control during this phase.

References - Web Sites

www.eifflander.com	Engines and CL wire
www.clubtamaran.com	Engines and CL accessories
www.bucks-composites.com	Epoxy/glass materials
www.apcprop.com	Props
www.justengines.co.uk	Engines and accessories
www.heckscher.co.uk	Spring steel wire
www.densmodelsupplies.co.uk	CL accessories and Profile W'man parts
www.fighteraces.co.uk	Epoxy paint
www.belairkits.com	Cut parts and Brodak agent

www.technohobby.com.ua — Engines and accessories
www.nclra.org — CL racing news
www.brodak.com — CL accessories
www.ema-models.co.uk — Jelutong wood
www.eliminatorprops.com — Glass and Carbon Props

References -Email Addresses

mike.edgerton@btinternet.com — 3D printed control line handles
tgoodger@hotmail.co.uk — Plan copies

Reference articles

Faster Phantoms, parts 1 & 2, Aeromodeller July/August 1996
Turtle FAI team racer, Aeromodeller, November 1973
Control line fuel tanks, Aeromodeller Annual 1967-68

WEATHERMAN PLAN

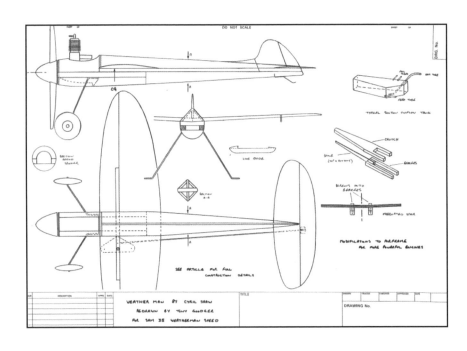

PROFILE WEATHEMAN PLAN

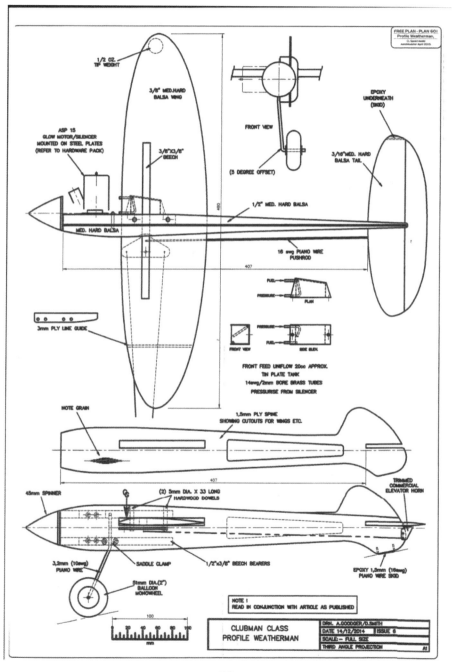

Something Old, Something New, Something - Egyptian?
(Roger Simmonds explains!)

Roger shares his love of classic aeromodelling with a parallel interest in computer-aided design (CAD); here he tells us how the two came together when he decided to build an unusual F/F design - the 'Scarab'.

"First, here's a little bit about myself. I can't remember a time when I wasn't making models of one sort or another. I used to shop for bits at Bunce's of Fareham and later came under the spell of Eric Coates after reading his series in the 'Aeromodeller' on F/F scale. Moving to Cambridge, I joined Ray Malmström's club at Impington College before taking a break in the early 90's to pursue a career.

Twenty years on and I've picked up the threads again, both building models and editing the Impington MAC newsletter. Slowly taking shape in the shed is a Coates-designed Airco DH.9A 'Nine-Ack' which will be finished - one day! Drawing plans on the computer is something I've just picked up – it's not rocket science (although for work, I did once read a paper in Norway at a Symposium on European Rocket and Balloon Programmes and Related Research, and found that even Rocket Science isn't rocket science!) – but with Terry King and Andrew Moorehouse both in our club, and they really *can* draw, I rate myself as just a CAD dabbler!"

Bitten by a Scarab at Old Warden

I bumped into Tim Gray at Old Warden back in May 2014. He was flying a Scarab, a model quite new to me then, and I was immediately intrigued. Narrow, with a deep fuselage, the model looked organic and seemed to flow from spinner to tail.

You see so many derivative designs, but this one stood out. Tim had added a D/T for F/F and flew it with a Dart up front. It seemed too that there was something *right* about this model, and a perfect fit with the spirit of flying FF at Old Warden.

Tim Gray's Scarab

Do you remember the first time you saw an E-type Jaguar, and thinking that you'd seen nothing like it? Well, for me, the experience was a bit like that. On getting back home I looked online and found not only the plan but also a print wood scan. Clearly, it was a builder's model and, with a characteristic banana fuselage, quite a challenge to cover too, no doubt.

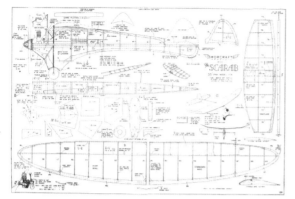

Designed by Albert Hatfull (of Keil Kraft Achilles, Ajax and Senator fame), it dated to 1949, when Albert was no longer designing for Eddie Keil but freelancing for Elite and Worcraft.

In an interview given to SAM35 he said that the Scarab had begun as a design exercise and wasn't intended for kitting, *"But I sent the design to Worcraft and to my surprise they actually did kit it, although it took a long while to work it out. I mean, the old Junior 60 is a bit of a workhorse. You couldn't say it was pretty. But I can still look at the Scarab and say to myself, 'Yes, I like that'."*

When compared to so many other designs the Scarab is a breath of fresh air. Over a period of weeks I kept returning to Albert's plan. Of typical AH quality, it's a delight and contains a *lot* of detail. But would it convert to electric power and could it be flown

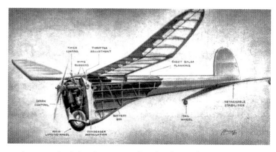

guided rather than FF? Yes, I thought, probably, but as I looked at the printwood scan I'd downloaded I was struck by just how many pieces there were to replicate. More to the point, the image quality wasn't up to much. It looked as though at least three formers were missing and had been roughly sketched in.

Albert and the Scarab

Then the thought occurred to me that I could redraw it and create a plan to complement the original. I could get the pieces laser cut and have nice crisp formers and ribs to work with. It wasn't something I'd done before, but being able to share the finished result with club mates made it seem that bit more worthwhile.

Looking round for a drawing package I found *'DraftSight'* from Dassault Systèmes. It's free to download and from the people behind *'SolidWorks'* (MM: *they're also owners of the full-fat 'CATIA' system used for designing 1/1 real* aircraft). If you haven't come across it then SolidWorks is a superb professional 3D

CAD package, while *DraftSight* is essentially 2D but, for what I had in mind, just the thing.

Learning Curve(s)

Now there's always some frustration in learning to use new software because you know it can do all this fancy stuff, but you don't quite know how to drive it. So I set aside just half an hour a day to fiddle about and learn the tools. By the end of a fortnight I felt ready to begin in earnest.

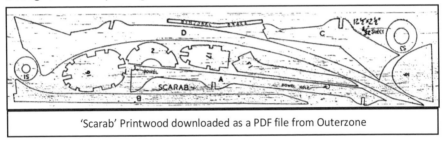

'Scarab' Printwood downloaded as a PDF file from Outerzone

There's a useful trick you can do with *DraftSight* and that is to drag in a .pdf or .jpg as a background image or layer. From then on you're able to draw over it, as though you'd placed a piece of tracing paper on top. In this way I was able to sketch some key lines and begin to take measurements. At a later stage, you can hide the background and once more see the wood for the trees.

The CAD conversion process at a glance

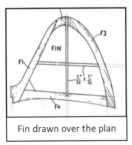

Fin drawn over the plan

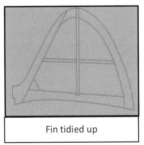

Fin tidied up

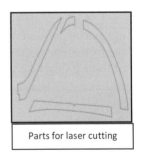

Parts for laser cutting

Recreating the formers

The formers are printed at odd angles to fit the original printwood and are distinctly sketchy in places; I was sure that as I copied each one I'd be adding in small errors – not good! There was, however, an alternative; I could grab the size of each former from the fuselage plan and re-create it, rather as Albert must have done in the first place. The first step in this process is to draw a fair outline over the original fuselage drawing, using the CAD 'spline' tool (it creates a smooth curve that passes through or near a set of chosen points) and straight lines - not that there are many straight lines on a Scarab! Then, measuring the height and width of each, the formers themselves can be drawn as elliptical arcs, one above the other. *(MM: I imagine that this is the CAD equivalent of laying a paper plan onto a sheet of balsa and pricking round the outline with a pin!)*

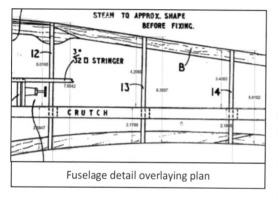

Fuselage detail overlaying plan

Placing the stringers proved a real headache and almost scuttled the project, but there were clues on the cut wood scan even though some formers were missing. I wanted the stringers to flow and felt they should be concentrated where the curvature was greater and reflect the banana shape of the model. In the end I looked at the angles formed by the stringer notches on four key formers and worked from them, interpolating for the missing formers. Now, spoiler alert, look away now if you're not

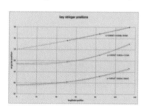

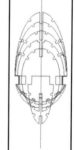

comfortable with spreadsheets! Microsoft Excel actually came in very useful when calculating the uncertain angular and lengthwise positions of intermediate formers on the plan by interpolating them between the known position of the four key formers – the graph is based upon some formulae I developed to achieve this. *(MM: Well, I must admit that my brain was starting to hurt a little at this point, but it's certainly an impressive marriage between modern technology and a great vintage design!)*

Wing Ribs – Rare or Well-Done?

Albert Hatfull provides this *'typical wing section'*, but what is it? Well, it's under-cambered, but it also has an unusual flat section leading to the trailing edge - could it be the Eiffel 431 from Ron Warring's own Airfoil Sections? This is what Warring has to say about that:

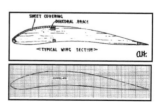

"It is surprising that the Eiffel sections are not used more widely by modellers for they give extremely good results at low Reynolds Numbers. The Eiffel 431 is similar to the Eiffel 400 but has a higher value of C_L maximum and so should appeal. C_L maximum is about 1.28 at 14 degrees angle of attack. C_D minimum is, unfortunately, rather high at 0.0193 and occurs at -5 degrees angle of attack. L/D maximum is 21.4, at 0 degree angle of attack when the lift coefficient is 0.5. The centre of pressure travel is quite reasonable, 45 per cent of the chord from the leading edge at L/D maximum moving to 31 per cent at C_L maximum."

Final Preparations

Once all the parts are drawn they can be pulled together into panels - these are the same in concept as the original printwood - ready for the files to be sent off for pre-processing and laser cutting. Several balsa panels are needed: 1/16" for ribs, 3/32" for formers and 1/8" for trailing edges, and there's a panel for ply parts too. I added some guidance comments for the laser-guys for the target weight of each panel. However, as we all know, wood selection is time consuming and expensive and not every laser shop is willing to take it on. The endplate rudders, for example, really need to be from C-grain balsa to provide stiffness, but it is unlikely you'll be able to specify this. Something else that I found useful was to add an extra cut line below each rib, so that once I'd extracted the ribs themselves I could glue these pieces at the correct stations along a building board; covered with 0.5mm ply they produced a perfectly contoured wing-building jig!

The Last Stage - Laser Cutting

The drawing process took a while, what with having to first learn how to use *DraftSight* then later on struggling with rib and stringer placement. However, at the back of my mind I kept thinking *"This is all worthwhile because getting the parts laser cut will be easy."* The first laser-cutting company I used proved that I was wrong – can you believe that corresponding ribs from each wing panel, and therefore cut from the *same* file, didn't match, resulting in all the balsa going into the bin? Fortunately I then found another company (*Manzano Laser in the USA*) who could cut panels from my drawings. Typically, I send them the files from *DraftSight* by email and get an email back next day to say they're on

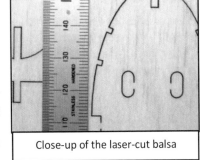

Close-up of the laser-cut balsa

the way back with USPS, here's the link for parcel tracking and the bill will be so much, which I settle with PayPal. After one to three weeks, (HM Customs can be a bottle-neck), the panels arrive. They are cut from Bud Nosen balsa, the quality is good and the precision is first class.

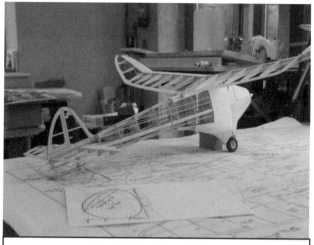

I can get away with flying my Scarab on throttle and rudder only, but I did have extra kits cut with added elevator, and these can fly even in a bit of wind. Recently, since very little effort is involved, I scaled the original drawings to 150% and had Manzano cut two sets for a 52.5" span version."

Roger's Scarab on the bench

Your Editor's fascination with Scarabs!

Scarabs are interesting things! The original Scarabs were sacred flying dung-beetles and their image was used as a decoration on amulets and seals in ancient Egypt, long before even Pontius was a pilot. Those amulets (and the original dung beetles!) survive in large numbers today. The inscriptions on the charms have been an important source of information for historians of the ancient world, in rather the same way that vintage plans are for SAM35 members!

'Scarab' has also been used as a name for aircraft, aircraft engines, boats and those cute three-wheeled Scammell prime movers used by the RAF and others back in the 1950s and 60s – so its connection with aviation is a strong one. Scammell named the successor to their Mechanical Horse using a crafty alliterative pun, 'Sc-ammell Sc-Arab', referring to a hardy type of horse, rather than to its beetle-like bonnet shells, which were in fact originally designed as rear roof corners for a Bedford bus!

A COMET GULL REBORN
(by Tom Baron)

Since my early teen years I've been interested in making broken things work again; between building stick and tissue model planes, I was always on the lookout for clapped-out motor bikes and Cushman motor scooters to fettle. I sometimes mounted a 'midnight requisition' plan to bring home abandoned motorised things to put in running order, but they always seemed to blow clouds of blue smoke when running, so when my modelling friend Noal Hess said that he'd uncovered an old rubber-powered plane that could use a home, I said: "Sign me up!"

Noal, a builder of museum quality quarter-scale planes, presented me with the tattered remains of a 42 inch wingspan 'Gull', kitted in 1942 by Comet Models and designed by Carl Goldberg. Noal always kept detailed notes of his projects and told me that he built the Gull in 1943 and flew it on the salt flats west of Salt Lake City, Utah. Its old tissue covering was in shreds, but the wood was remarkably sound and straight - that old Ambroid glue must have been made to a special formula back in those days!

I decided that the best course of action was to convert the plane into a three-channel R/C flier, thus helping to keep it in good condition and not lose it to thermals. There was plenty of wood in the rudder for a control surface, but I used a strip elevator instead of cutting into the stabilizer in case I ever wanted to bring it back to F/F status.

After carefully removing the old tissue and replacing a few struts I used a double covering technique: first some .0015" Mylar went on to protect against moisture, followed by water-tightened tissue, then finally a spray of acrylic sealer. I left the hand-made balsa wheels alone because they still have salt stains on them from the flats - a moist finger will give me a taste of vintage salt from 1943!

Something that I noticed after consulting an AMA plan of the Gull was that on my model not all the wing ribs were lined up at 90 degrees to the spars. Was the wing warped? No! Could it be sloppy building? No way at all, Noal was far too careful a builder for that. I came to the conclusion that the wing had been intentionally built with the left panel advanced forward in order to offset propeller torque and to aid in a right hand glide.

The restored airframe weighed in at 152 grams and the electric equipment, 8x4 GWS propeller and two cell LiPo battery gave me an all up weight of about nine ounces - not light, but certainly good for a wing of 182 square inches and a rearward CG so that the stabilizer could assist as a lifting body. I completed the Gull in 2009; not long after it featured in the FLYING MODEL Magazine, and I'm happy to say that it still flies occasionally in my local park on calm days!

HEROES FOR HIRE: The Air-Commodore's Last Case
(by Lord Bertie Lissie)

I say there, what-ho! If you've read any of those books about Biggles you'll know that Air-Commodore Raymond was Biggles' chief in the mob – frightfully clever chap! When he left the RAF after the last beastliness he joined the Met as head of their Air Police to catch blighters using aircraft for their monkey-business. He even recruited Biggles and his team (including me, myself, personally y'know!) to help.He retired again to write his life-story but had a dashed 'D' Notice slapped on him, so with nothing to do he got as bored as a bally Teredo worm without a ship's plank to nibble.

Well, blow me down if he didn't go and set up a new outfit doing hush-hush stuff for the Ministry of Defence – d'y'know what I mean? Well, he earned a packet from that and decided to retire again, so he'd just sold the business to yours truly and good old Algy (The Hon. Algernon Lacey, super chappie) when some rum cove from Buckminster tricked him into doing a final job for the British Model Flying Air Police – what a bounder, eh? Well, here's what happened in Raymond's last and most baffling case – he called it 'HEROES for HIRE'! Pip-pip, toodle-oo and Tally-Ho, old bean!

The Gramophone was playing at full volume, blaring out a rather modern 'pop' tune that reverberated around the corrugated iron roof of the empty hangar. An attractive woman of about 35 lay slumped across the battered sofa in the corner, clutching an empty bottle of absinthe and weeping as she wailed along with the song that was playing.

The Air-Commodore peered doubtfully around the hangar door. He'd been dragged out of his comfortable retirement to do this last job on the promise of being awarded the Manny Medal – nothing else would have tempted him to do it, he mused, cursing himself for being so vain and so weak....

Listening to the ghastly racket coming from inside the hangar, he was certain that this was the rendezvous he'd been instructed to keep, even though his ears were hurting as the woman bawled tunelessly along with the record:

"...he's gotta be sure and it's gotta be soon and he's gotta be larger than life, I need a hero, I'm holding out for a hero 'til the end of the night..."

Raymond smiled to himself - yes, this was his target! He mentally reviewed the case notes he'd been reading in the BMFAP clubhouse that afternoon. The lady (named Samantha) had been approached by the TCB, a shadowy organization operating on the fringes of the tarmac occupied by the model flying fraternity.

They'd wanted her help to legitimize their activities and so had approached her to represent them, but she'd been undecided. However, the TCB had kept pressing her with their pamphlets and presentations so that over time they'd drawn her deeper and deeper towards their clutches until she felt quite spindizzy...

She actually rather liked some of their ideas, but she still had a duty to her old supporters. Leading a double life is a tough call, so she'd decided to appeal to the BMFAP for protection against these insurgents. She'd asked them for the services of a Hero to protect her from further pressure while she thought things over for herself. Raymond chuckled sardonically to himself – if there was a Hero available, it wouldn't be him – after all, he was now in his thirteenth decade, but he knew a few chaps from the old days who might be able to assist a lady in distress.

"I say, old thing, don't take on so!" he soothed, easing himself into the hangar and gently pulling the gramophone's plug from the wall-socket on his way past. He patted the overwrought lass on the shoulder as blessed silence reigned again.

"A sniff of this will buck you up..." He un-stoppered the small bottle of Dr J. Collis Browne's Chlorodyne that he always carried for such emergencies, and waved it under her nose – "and do please use my hanky!"

Samantha took his embroidered and monogrammed silk handkerchief, blew her nose copiously into it then handed it back to him. "Thank you," she snivelled. "I suppose you're going to arrest me for collaboration – I wouldn't blame you."

The Air-Commodore looked puzzled. "No, I'm certainly not here for that - but I'd really like to know why you feel the need for protection at all - are these people that dangerous?" he asked, gingerly gripping his sodden handkerchief between thumb and forefinger.

"Well," she replied, "I know that the TCB are counter-revolutionaries" (Raymond nodded to himself - these were definitely some sort of control-line fanatics – dangerous chaps, as he'd suspected!) "But I'm stuck in the middle between them and the BMFAP - I don't like it so I'm passing the buck upstairs to you chaps, and I do need some top cover while I sort myself out!"

"I see" he replied, "well, I think I can assist you there; I've got a portfolio of possible, er, Heroes for you, any of whom could help, and all you have to do is pick the one you want!"

He extracted a slim brochure marked *'Heroes for Hire Agency Ltd'* from his raincoat pocket, sat down beside Samantha (whom we'll now call Sam for short), and turned to the first page. She peered at the picture, then read through the first CV with mounting excitement – it said:

HERO #1: 'BILL BARNES'

'Bill has had a long and successful career with us. His adventures as a multi-talented aircraft designer, builder, pilot and aerial tactician – not to mention his ability to improvise whilst sticking to good engineering principles - are well-documented in the Air Trails magazines published between 1934 -39.

Bill first flew as an airmail pilot, then took time out for a solo flight around the world, after which he returned home to found his own airport and airline.'

"Coo, he must be worth a few bob!" gasped Sam, powdering her nose vigorously. "Is he available? He looks like the sort of rugged type that I need!"

Unfortunately, after making some rapid enquiries on his portable telex machine Raymond discovered that Bill was currently away on a secret mission in the Orient with his new 'Charger' aeroplane, testing its radio navigation, amphibious landing gear, powerful hidden diesel engines, single-blade propellers and stainless steel wings against his arch-enemy Mordechai Murphy, so he wasn't going to be available any time soon. Sam sighed with disappointment and turned the page.

HERO #2: 'DUSTY AYRES'

'Dusty is another long-term but somewhat lightly-used consultant that we are pleased to offer for those more improbable missions. His noteworthy adventures were recorded in his own memoir *'Dusty Ayres and His Battle Birds'* in July 1934, published by Popular Publications. Although he did fight in WW1, his more recent missions saw him in Asia, seeking out his arch-enemy 'Fire-Eyes and his Black Invaders', who'd decided to attack and conquer America single-handedly. Dusty and his three chums joined forces with 'Agent 10', an undercover American intelligence officer, to save the free world from Fire Eyes and his villains'.

"Did he succeed?" asked Sam. "Well, we're not sure," replied the Air-Commodore, "because he disappeared without trace halfway through the campaign with a terminal circulation problem". "Oh the poor dear," sympathized Sam, "did he suffer from a weak heart?"

"No, he had a weak scriptwriter and even weaker sales..." murmured Raymond, "But let's move on – as Bessie Banks once said, the best is yet to come!" On the next page they found...

HERO #3: 'G-8'

'G-8, although he's sometimes confused with the international G8 forum that 'solves' global challenges, is very different from them – for a start, he's got a little

dash and he's not just another WW1 ex-fighter pilot – he's also been an espionage agent! Working with his 'Battle Ace' chums – Nippy's the small clever one, Bull's the big, strong, dozy one and Battle is their butler - he not only fought the Boche Army but also faced up to some of the Kaiser's weirdest allies, including a giant spider, beast-men, a Martian fighting alongside the chaps in pikelhaubes and, to top it off, a squadron of German pilots returning from the grave as zombies!'

Looking hopeful, Raymond asked eagerly: "What do you think of that, then?"

"I think," remarked Sam, "that although these chaps might have been top-drawer fighting men back in the 1930s, it's unlikely that they'd be up to dealing with the TCB today, even if you could persuade them to try - they'd be facing a bunch of desperate fanatics!" The Air-Commodore could see her point, so he began flipping through the brochure towards its later pages to find someone more 'du jour'.

HERO #4: 'BATTLER BRITTON'

"Now, how about Battler Britton?" he asked; "He's a bit more recent..." Sam shrugged her elegant shoulders, unimpressed by Battler's obviously 1940s vintage - where were the modern heroes when she needed one? "What did he do?" she asked, stifling a yawn.

"Well, he was very famous in the 1960s and 70s" began Raymond, "WW2 was still within recent memory, so Hereward Robert Britton's stories of daring with a squadron of plucky Brits versus evil Nazis were all the rage – he was even featured in a revival series in the 1980s so he's certainly a bit more recent, but before you ask," he continued hurriedly as he skimmed Battler's CV, "he was last heard of fighting the Germans in the Sahara in 1942..."

"Next!" demanded Sam, clearly becoming worried by their lack of progress, the few pages left in the brochure and the hint of dawn outside the hangar – she needed protection before the TCB came looking for her at daybreak.

HERO #5: 'MAJOR JAMES BIGGLESWORTH'

Raymond closed the booklet – he didn't need it for this one. "Of course, there's always my old chum Biggles, former air ace, founding member of the Air Police and currently looking for a job like this. He's had a hard time recently. He's actually having to claim age-related housing benefit after a messy separation from his protégé Ginger; the young cad stole Biggles' life savings and his Auster Autocrat and flew off to live with their former arch-enemy Erich von Stalhein. Biggles could do with the money, you know; he's sleeping rough in the hangar here most of the time."

"So how old is 'young' Ginger, then?" asked Sam, fearing the worst. "Oh, he'd be about 99 now," replied Raymond, inspecting his polished brogues closely.

"...and Biggles is...?" she asked pointedly. The Air Commodore coughed, thought for a moment then admitted that the former commander of 666 Squadron would be 119 the following week.

"I don't think he's at all suitable!" snapped Sam, unimpressed. "I've read that he always makes his team spilt up on every adventure and search separately for something or other in the jungle or the Sahara, and that's when the real trouble starts! He's not a team player! Who else have you got in that brochure of yours?"

Raymond showed her Johnnie Wingco's profile, the master pilot from 1958 whose exploits were reported in the 'Knockout' comic every week (verdict – too much of a showoff, flying his Gloster Javelin at zero feet inverted along the runway)

Dan Dare from the Eagle got short shrift too: (verdict - she actually preferred Digby, Dare's amiable, tubby aide, as Dare himself seemed to be over-obsessed with a little green man sitting on a Frisbee and might desert her to chase after him at the drop of a ray-gun; however, she wasn't sure that Digby would be able to resist the lardy cakes that the TCB would tempt him with).

"That just leaves two possibilities" grunted the Air-Commodore through gritted teeth. This wasn't going well.

"How about Fixit Wright from the 'Flying Models' magazine? He's really good at getting into, er sorry, getting *out* of ridiculous situations, such as deliberately flying his model over a forest in the evening, losing it, then borrowing someone else's Cessna 310 to look for it at $300 an hour".

"What a pillock!" exclaimed Sam, "I'm amazed that those pretty young things he hangs around with put up with his antics!" Raymond felt obliged to explain that Fixit was believed to be the beneficiary of a substantial Trust Fund, so that was probably why he remained popular with the girls.

"Oh, I see" said Sam brightly, "they obviously know that he's very well endowed...."

Raymond closed the brochure with a sigh, excused himself and walked outside to think. Should he suggest the obvious candidate for Sam, or would it lead to more trouble? He leaned against the hangar wall. Reaching into his coat pocket for his tortoiseshell cigarette-case, he selected a Strand (he never felt alone when smoking one, but he did rather prefer Balkan Sobranies), lit it with the Dunhill lighter he'd been given when he retired for the third time so many years ago and drew deeply upon the cigarette. After all, this was his last job, and his last chance to finish his 100-year-long career on a high note. He had

nothing to lose, and a lot to gain. Why not? Flicking the dimp into the undergrowth, he returned to Sam and made his final proposal.

"Sam, the only other possible candidate is still appearing regularly in a popular monthly magazine, so he's really up-to-date" he told her cautiously, "He's a very stern disciplinarian. He doesn't fight physically but one look from him is guaranteed to turn an insurgent's knees to jelly. He won't put up with any nonsense, insists upon processes and procedures being followed and can frighten trouble-makers into immobility simply by demanding a hazard analysis and mitigation strategy for whatever naughtiness they're thinking of getting up to – and he's young and attractive too, I'm told."

"He sounds perfect!" gushed Sam, "Where is he, I'd love to meet him!" As she spoke, a door carefully disguised as the entrance to a boot-cupboard swung open behind the sofa and her Hero-to-be strolled into the hangar. He was wearing his usual immaculately-tailored grey suit, looking perfectly–groomed, confident, self-possessed, lithe and alert. His amber eyes locked onto hers, and Sam immediately felt reassured. He sprang onto the sofa and spoke using the voice-of-command he was renowned for.

"Sam, you mustn't worry about the TCB. I've been covertly monitoring their activities for months, and your reports have been invaluable! It was very brave of you to deal with such radicals alone, but now you need some help.

"If I'm going to be the official conduit between you and them" (Sam nodded enthusiastically) "I'll pursue any deviation from the terms of reference you agree with them, and make sure they behave themselves and do exactly what YOU say or I'll be on their case – that's a promise!"

Sam blushed and put her arm around him. "Oh thank you!" she simpered, "I'm so grateful!"

"I say, hold on a moment" bristled the Air-Commodore, "What actually **IS** this TCB organization up to? I'm feeling completely out of the loop here!"

"Sir," replied Sam's New Hero, "they're the *'Tethered Car Brigade'*, well-known activists in Sam's circles and intent upon gaining Momentum for their brand of control-line activity" he replied. "I'm off to start work on the appropriate risk assessment at once," he said, winking at Sam as he leapt from the sofa and made his way back to his office: "I'll be in touch – and watch out for an interesting picture!"

"Wait!" she called after him. "Who are you? I don't even know your name!"

He turned back: "The Quality Inspector is at your service, Ma'am!" he said gravely as he bowed and then slipped like a grey shadow through the door of his office to start work.

A moment later, a photograph appeared on Raymond's cell-phone. He rarely used it, preferring the privacy of a good old-fashioned concrete kiosk, but for once it had his full attention as he studied the covertly-taken picture from the Quality Inspector.

It was captioned **'TCB – the Inner Circle'** and for the first time he could see who they really were. He smiled to himself grimly and dialed the prearranged emergency number; the BMFAP Flying Squad would soon be on its way to sort this lot out!

...and the rest, as they say, is history!

Credits:

Gordon 'Gamma' Rae – for suggesting the original concept of an article about comic book heroes – it probably hasn't turned out quite as he expected...

SAM (35 years old), also known as **Samantha** - for being a good sport

The BMFA(P) - for hopefully being an even better sport

The TCB - for hopefully being the best sport of all!

The Quality Inspector - for ensuring good order and process adherence at all times

Acknowledgement is also made to all the authors, artist, artistes and publishers of their ownership of those excerpts from classic comics, books, advertisements, songs, products and articles used for review, study and comparison within this article.

THE YEARBOOK 16 PLANS-CHEST

I love studying plans, even when I know that I'll never build most of the models I look at. Why? I like to puzzle out how I'd set about building the model, what changes I might make, and most importantly, what was going on in the designer's head – you can learn a lot from that to use when designing and building other models.

Some of my SAM35 colleagues advised me to keep this section very short, or to even consider ditching it completely, but I couldn't do that – it wouldn't be a proper Yearbook without plans!

However, I've decided to focus on some of the wackier designs that don't usually get an airing, in the hope that you might just be inspired to build the Boehle Giant, or the Tandem R/C Bomber or even the rubber-powered Ornithopter!

To scratch a permanent itch left by my 40+ years working for Westland Helicopters there had to be some rotary-wing designs, and of course rubber-fanciers, Jetex aficionados, glider fans and control-line handlers are all catered for too. There are over thirty to enjoy, I hope they give you as much fun as I had selecting them!

Section 1: Ornithopters
Section 2: Control Line
Section 3: Rotary Wing
Section 4: Free-Flight Power
Section 5: Gliders
Section 6: Jetex
Section 7: Radio Control
Section 8: Rubber Power
Section 9: Tethered Car

These reduced-size plan images are offered for study and research: the original designer's and publisher's rights are fully acknowledged.

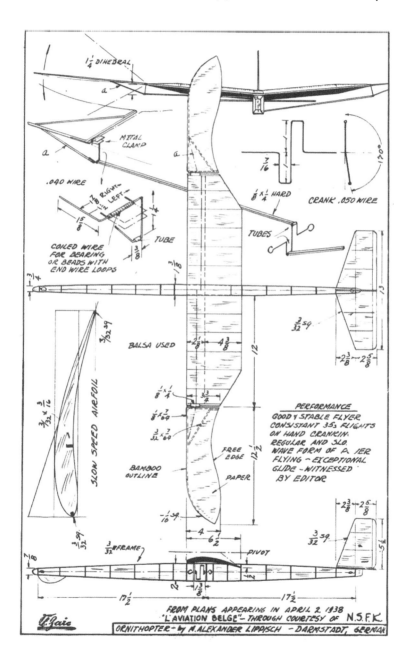

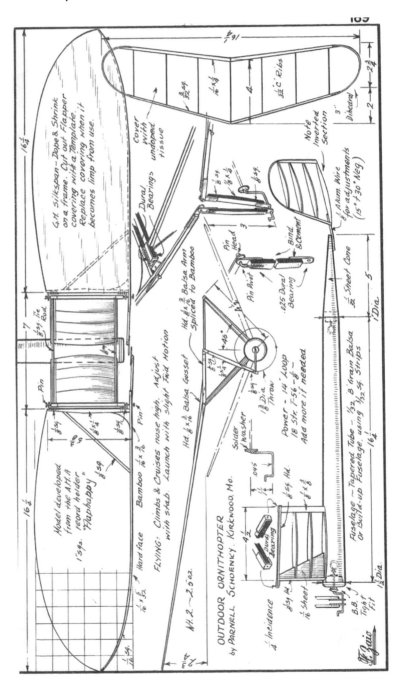

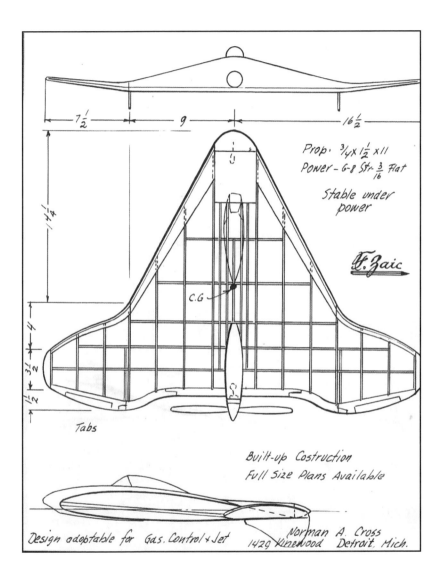

Prop. $\frac{3}{4} \times 1\frac{1}{2} \times 11$

Power - 6-8 Str. $\frac{3}{16}$ Flat

Stable under power

F. Zaic

C.G.

$7\frac{1}{2}$

9

$16\frac{1}{2}$

$4\frac{1}{4}$

4

$3\frac{1}{2}$

$\frac{1}{2}$

Tabs

Built-up Costruction
Full Size Plans Available

Design adaptable for Gas. Control + Jet

Norman A. Cross
1429 Kinewood Detroit. Mich.

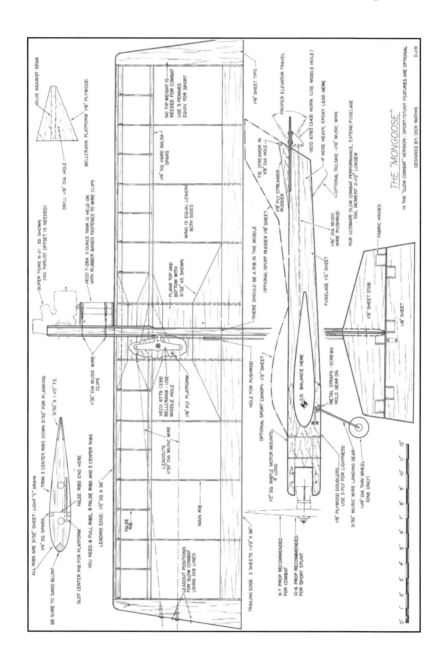

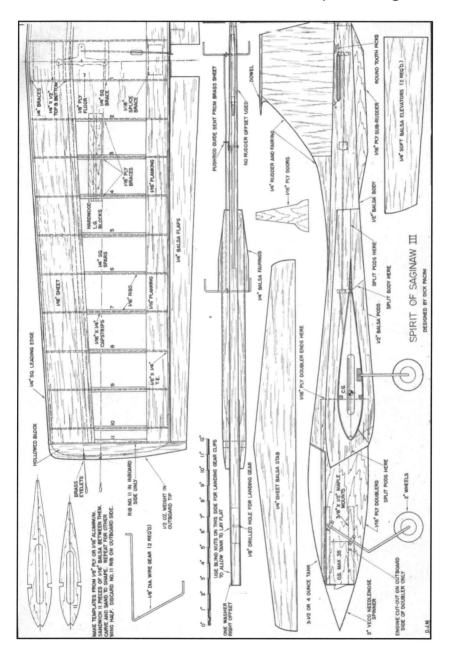

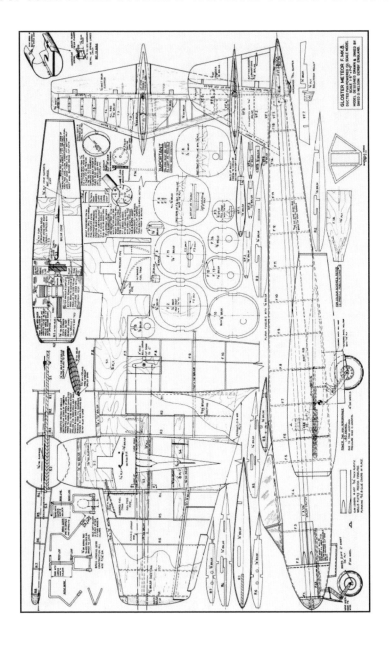

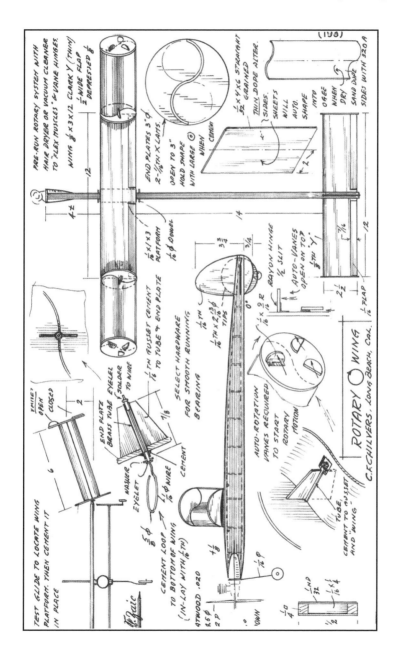

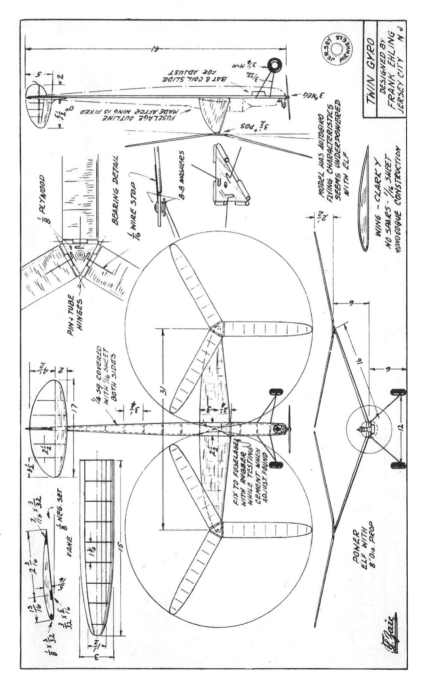

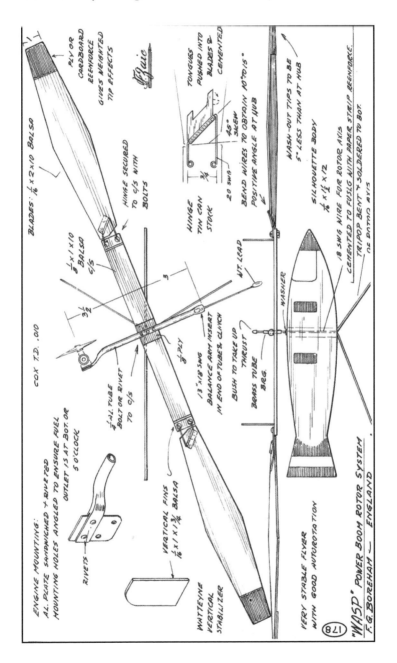

BLADES: $\frac{1}{16} \times 2 \times 10$ BALSA

PLY OR CARDBOARD REINFORCE GIVES WEIGHTED TIP EFFECTS

TONGUES PUSHED INTO BLADES & CEMENTED

$\frac{Blaïo}{}$

HINGE SECURED TO C/S WITH BOLTS

HINGE TIN CAN STOCK

45° SCREW

$\frac{3}{4}$

20 SWG

BEND WIRES TO OBTAIN 10°TO 15° POSITIVE ANGLE AT HUB

$\frac{1}{8} \times 1 \times 10$ BALSA C/S

$\frac{1}{8}$ PLY

$3\frac{1}{2}$

3

WT. LEAD

WASH-OUT TIPS TO BE 5° LESS THAN AT HUB

SILHOUETTE BODY $\frac{1}{16} \times 1\frac{1}{2} \times 12$

18 SWG WIRE FOR ROTOR AXIS

COX T.D. .010

$\frac{1}{4}$ INT. TUBE BOLT OR RIVET TO C/S

/3"x18 SWG BALANCE ARM INSERT IN END OF TUBES. CLINCH

BUSH TO TAKE UP THRUST

BRASS TUBE BRG.

WASHER

CEMENTED TO FUSLG WITH PAPER STRIP REINFORCE. TRIPOD BENT & SOLDERED TO BOT. OF ROTOR AXIS

ENGINE MOUNTING: AL. PLATE SANDWICHED & RIVETED MOUNTING HOLES ANGLED TO ENSURE FUEL OUTLET IS AT BOT. OR 5 O'CLOCK

RIVETS

VERTICAL FINS $\frac{1}{16} \times 1 \times 1\frac{3}{4}$ BALSA

WATTEYNE VERTICAL STABILIZER

VERY STABLE FLYER WITH GOOD AUTOROTATION

"WASP" POWER BOOM ROTOR SYSTEM
F. G. BOREHAM — ENGLAND.

178

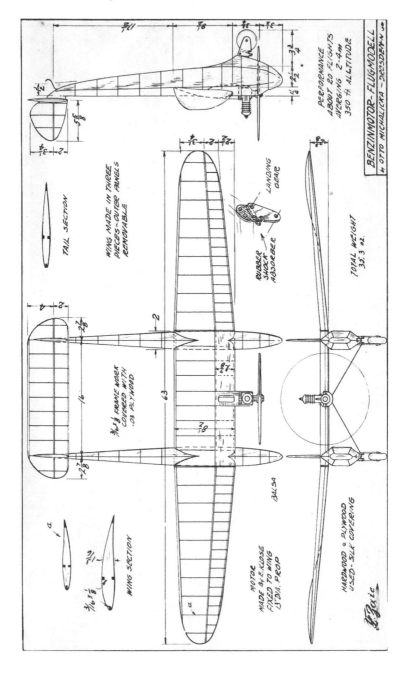

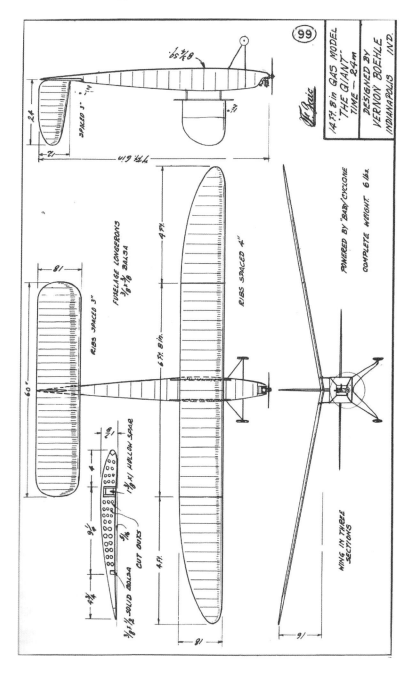

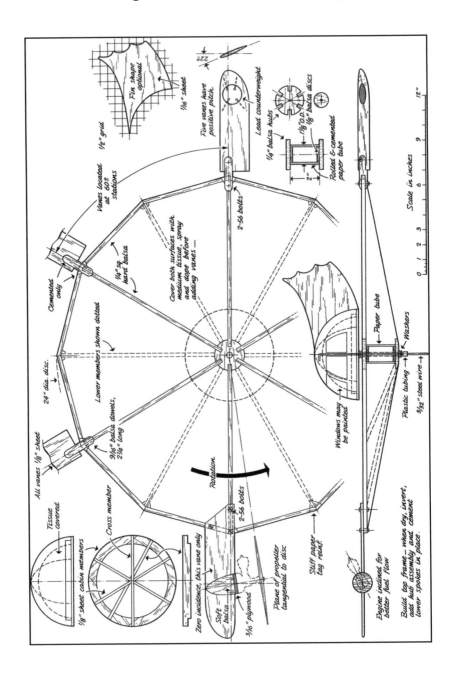

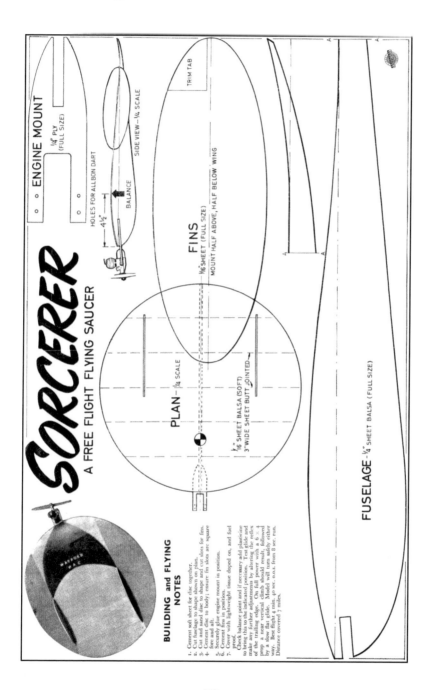

SORCERER

A FREE FLIGHT FLYING SAUCER

ENGINE MOUNT ¼" PLY (FULL SIZE)

HOLES FOR ALLBON DART

BALANCE

4½"

SIDE VIEW – ¼ SCALE

FINS ¹⁄₁₆" SHEET (FULL SIZE)

MOUNT HALF ABOVE, HALF BELOW WING

TRIM TAB

PLAN – ¼ SCALE

¹⁄₁₆" SHEET BALSA (SOFT)
3" WIDE SHEET BUTT JOINTED

FUSELAGE ¼" SHEET BALSA (FULL SIZE)

BUILDING and FLYING NOTES

1. Cement soft sheet for disc together.
2. Cut fuselage to shape shown on plan.
3. Cut and sand disc to shape and cut slots for fins.
4. Cement disc to body; ensure fin slots are square fore and aft.
5. Securely glue engine mount in position.
6. Cement fins in position.
7. Cover with lightweight tissue doped on, and fuel proof.

Check balance point and if necessary add plasticine to bring this to the indicated position. Test glide and make any further adjustments by altering the reflex of the trailing edge. On full power with a 6 × 4 prop a near vertical climb should result, followed by a slow flat glide. Model will turn safely either way. Best flight 4 min. 40 sec. o.o.s. from 9 sec. run. Distance covered 7 miles.

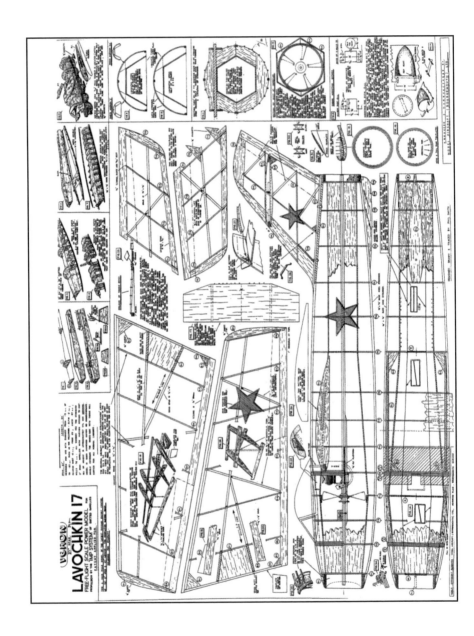

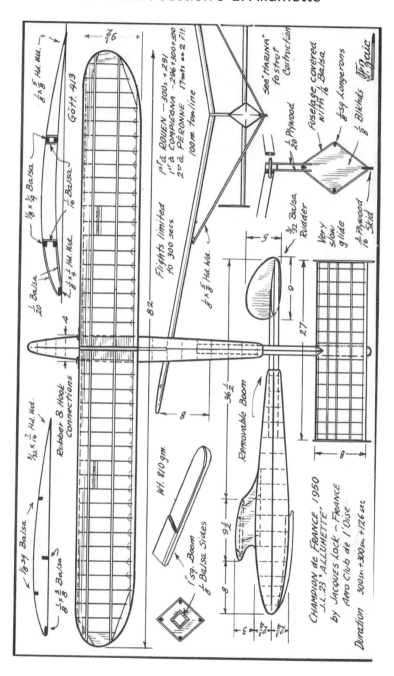

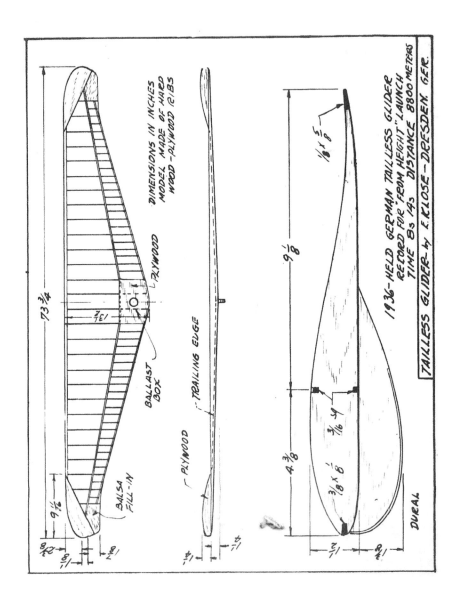

DIMENSIONS IN INCHES
MODEL MADE OF HARD
WOOD — PLYWOOD RIBS

PLYWOOD

BALLAST BOX

TRAILING EDGE

PLYWOOD

BALSA FILL-IN

73 3/4

13 1/2

9 1/2

3/2 5/2

1/8

1/8 1/7

1/4
1/7

1/8 × 1/8

9 1/8

4 3/8

3/16 4

3/8 × 1/8

1/2
1/7

1/2
1/4

DUREAL

1936 — HELD GERMAN TAILLESS GLIDER
RECORD FOR FROM HEIGHT "LAUNCH
TIME 8s 14s DISTANCE 8800 METERS

TAILLESS GLIDER by E. KLOSE — DRESDEN. GER.

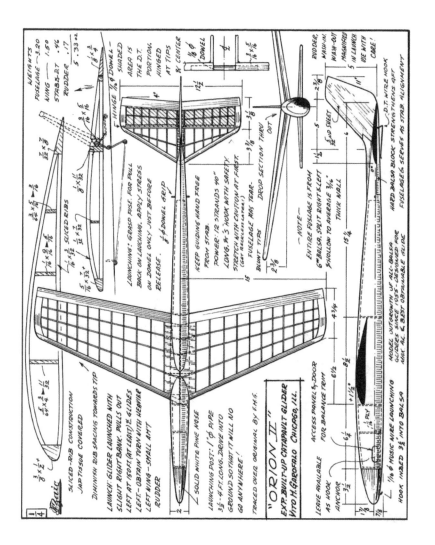

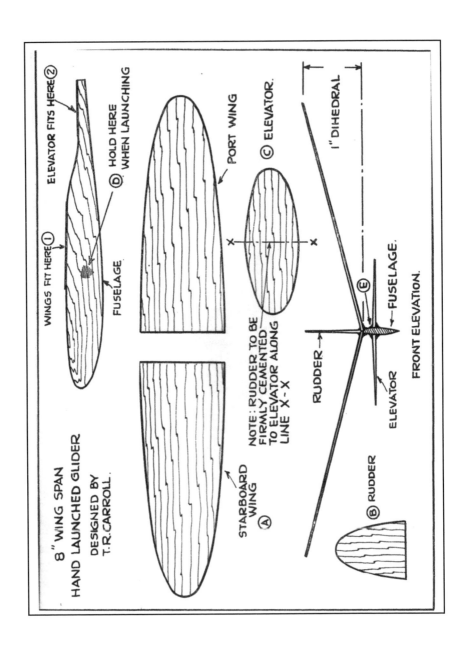

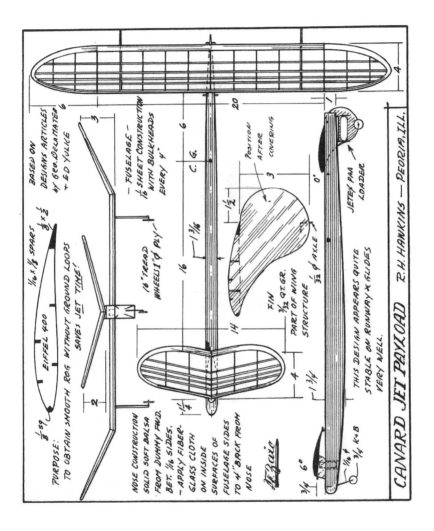

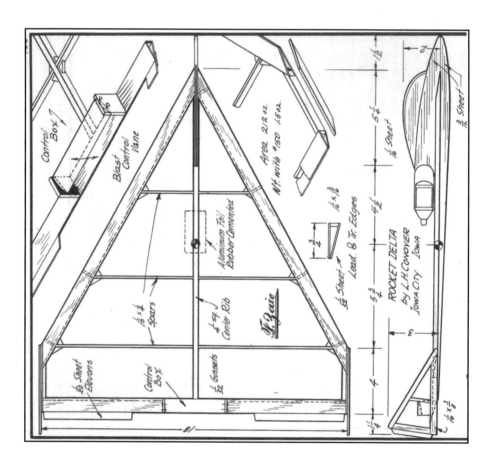

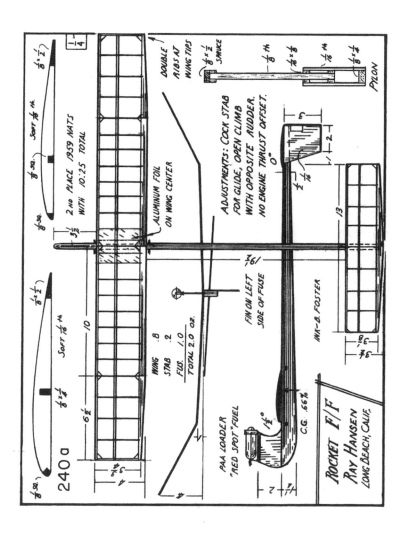

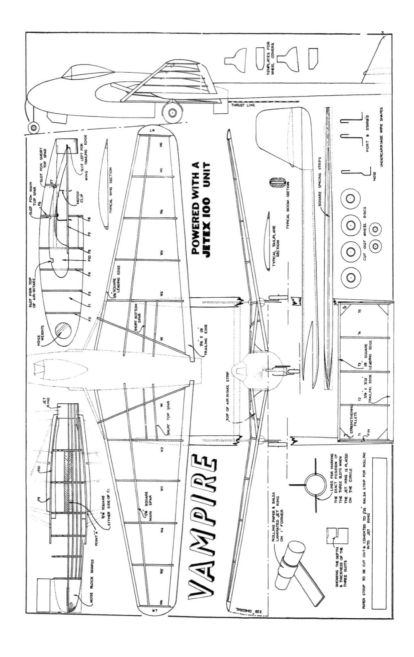

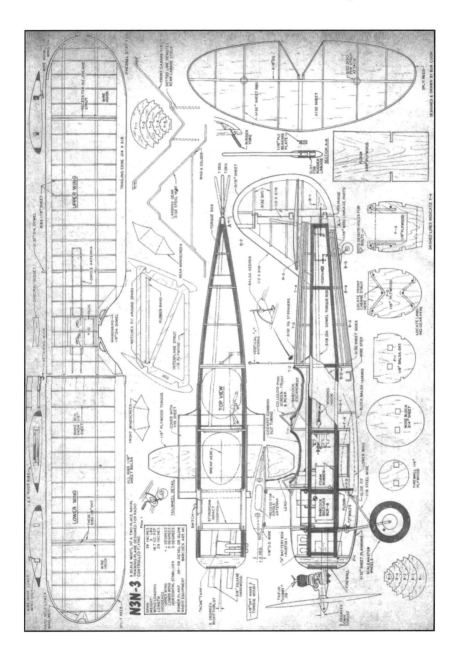

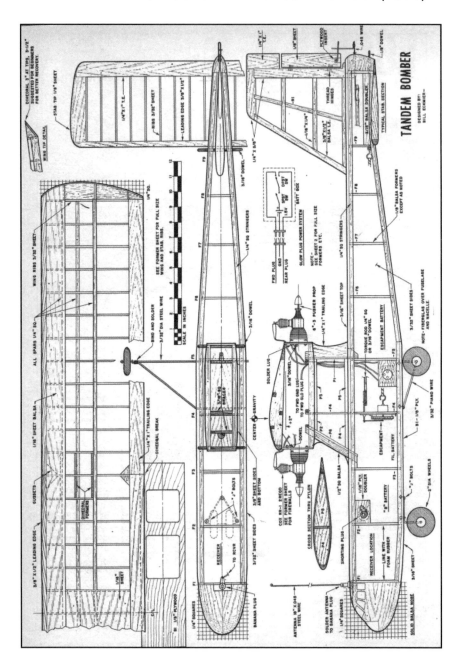

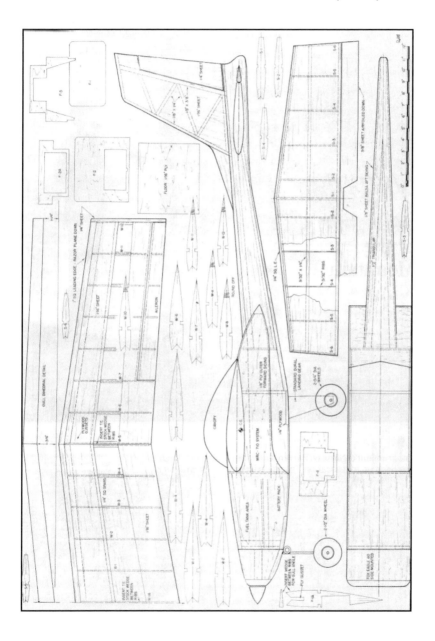

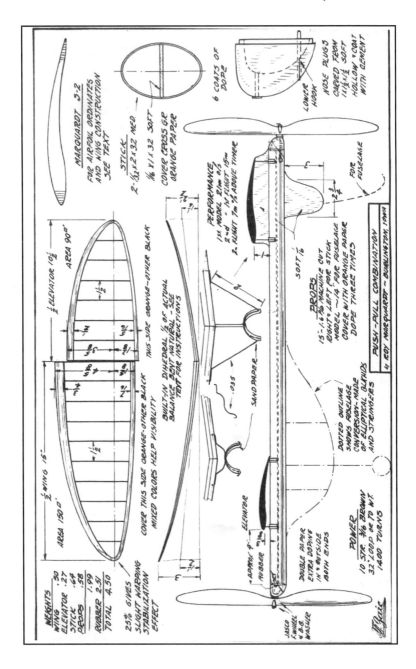

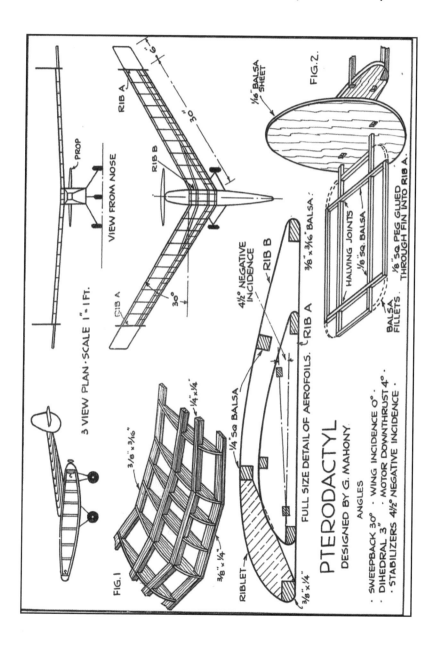

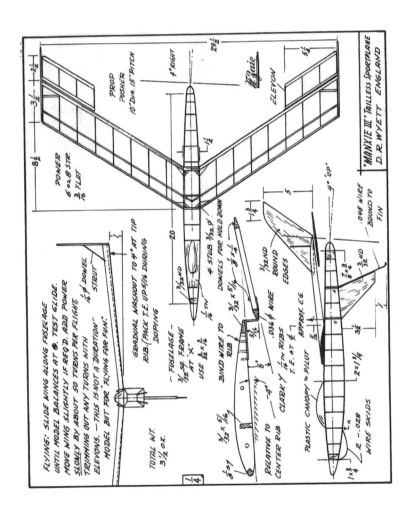

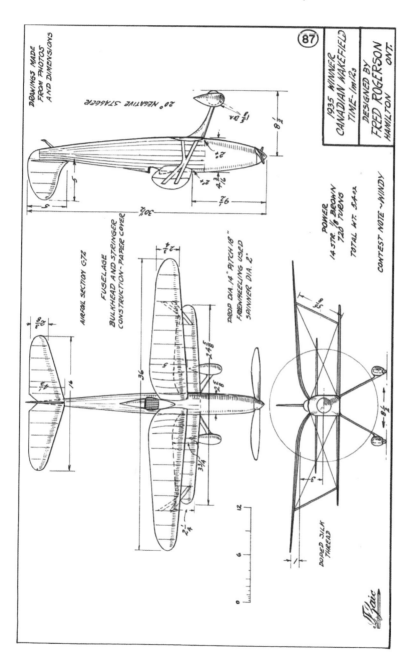

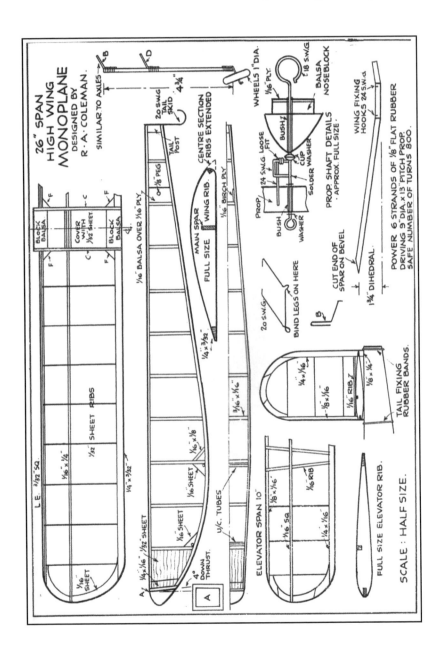

31: Tethered Car Section 9-1: Galeota 'AG' Midget (1942)

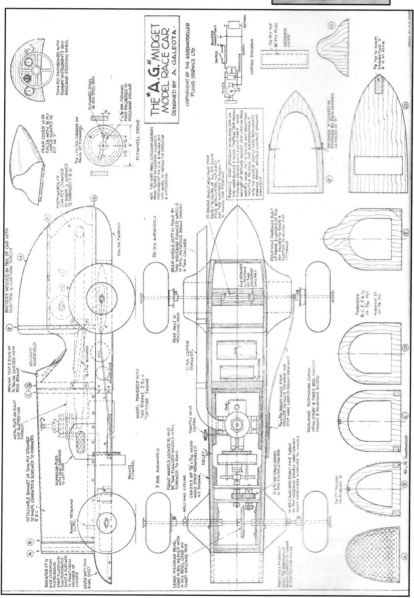

SAM35 YEARBOOK 16 – YOUR LANDING CARD

DATELINE AUGUST 14th 2018 - 08:00: YB16 TOUCHDOWN! The Quality Inspector and I were sitting at the breakfast table sharing a plate of Marmite soldiers, ready to start our regular weekly progress review - I was hoping this would be the last one before we sent the final draft to the printer.

All the material was scattered around us, either on paper or on the laptop, ready for his technical, literary and layout sign-off, or more likely, rejection. He'd clearly been looking forward to this moment immensely as he sat next to a huge wad of non-conformance forms with a sardonic smile on his face. He'd spent the whole day before our meeting in his office in the boot cupboard, reading through the material between naps and snacks, and undoubtedly finding fault – it's something he's very good at!

"What's the verdict?" I asked timidly. "Lots of errors to correct, I suppose. If you like, I'll take those forms from you now and get started on them right away." He pushed the pile of non-conformance reports towards me. "Have a look for yourself" he invited smugly, "it's truly astonishing!" So I leafed through the pile of forms with growing bewilderment as I found blank sheet after blank sheet, until I reached his summary on very last one, which read:

"Overall, not too bad for someone with no discernable track record in top-flight model aviation, Yearbook editing or anything else for that matter. There are a few rather lightweight pieces that you've probably written yourself, and there's an incurable desire to alter your contributors' articles to read smoothly where you presumed to find it necessary, but overall it seems like a reasonable-enough mix; of course, whether the members like it or not remains to be seen, they're sure to let you know!"

Later, when he'd retired to his laundry basket for a siesta, I sat and thought about what he'd said – it was pretty accurate, really. On the personal side, the most valuable and humbling experience I've had from editing this Yearbook has been the willingness of SAM members to write articles and send them to me on spec from the UK, Europe, America, Canada and South Africa with no guarantee of inclusion, trusting in the team here to do right by them and their work.

I know how hard devising, writing and finishing an article can be, and our contributors have spent significant amounts of their time and effort doing just that, their only motivation being a desire to spread the word about our kind of aeromodelling. Their efforts are what make this Yearbook what it is, so contributors all, please take a bow – the editorial team sincerely thanks and salutes you!

I must also give my heartfelt thanks to the other two members of the Yearbc editorial team who have given me immense encouragement, helpful (if sometime deservedly stern) criticism, useful suggestions and in particular, their valuable time.

Firstly, there's my wife Jane Nolting-May, who captured and organised the data, proof-read it, and double-checked articles for logical structure, chasing out all those faults I couldn't see for looking – a very valuable task well-performed indeed!

Secondly, (although he feels he should be first, of course) there's the Quality Inspector, aka Dr Nunu Blue Moon, who was (in his own opinion) the real power behind the whole project; he features regularly in my column 'Wind in the Wires' in the monthly SAM Speaks magazine, trying his best to keep me on the path of aeromodelling righteousness by forcing me to follow process, procedure and good engineering practice in my model building and flying, none of which come easily to me!

His response to most of what I do is usually "I can't believe it's not better!" but this time, remarkably, he seemed gruffly satisfied.

Thank you both – I couldn't have done it without you!

"Hmm – that undercarriage repair definitely looks bodged to me!"

If you'd like to add **your** comments to the QI's, then why not email him at QI@witw.org.uk and tell us how we did!